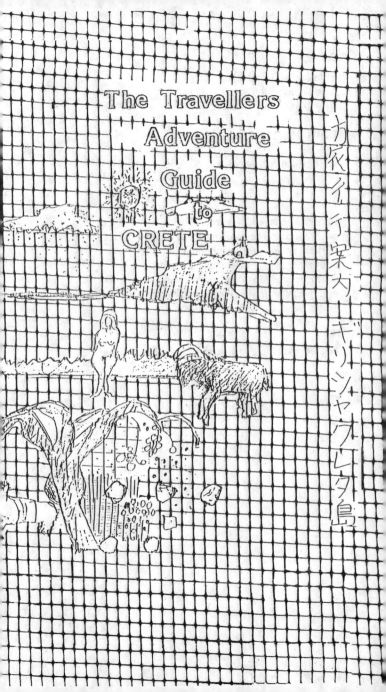

The Travellers Adventure Guide to CRETE

旅行案内 ギリシャクレタ島

Efstathiadis Group S.A.
Agiou Athanasiou Street,
GR - 145 65 Anixi, Attikis

ISBN 960 226 450 0

© Efstathiadis Group S.A. 1993

Printed and bound in Greece by Efstathiadis Group S.A.

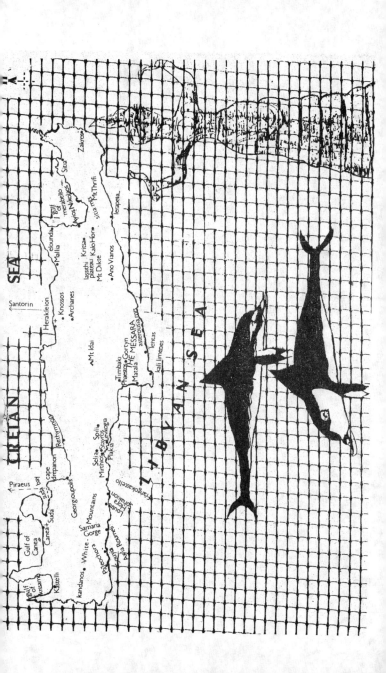

"Would that this were for Ireland"

This book is dedicated to

my Mother and Father
for peace in the 4 fields
and to the people of the Tropical Rainforest.

Many thanks to

Cecile, Jerry Whelan, A. Milne, M. O'Sullivan, Mona & Susanne,
George, Nikos, and the people of Crete.

Part One

Venetian Rethymnon

The Hostel was just off one of the busy shopping streets of the Cretan Town; I entered it through an Eastern style passageway, which revealed an old Turkish Courtyard with a large grapevine growing up from the centre of the yard-to the washing-lined rooftop rooms, about twenty feet above. Where there was maybe once a Fountain and Courtesans reposing (I fancied), there were now lines of sinks and the odour of washing powder, with hostelers of all ages and nationalities, taking showers, reading and writing and conversing, or just doing the washing; scantily clad girls coming and going to the washhouse; arrivals and departures in this, a Hedonistic but transient lifestyle, with the sound of 60's Pop creating a somewhat nostalgic air to the Place. Was this feeling I had, that of my lost youth? for it couldn't have been the young travellers lost happy times! - as they were still young, or maybe it was something I had felt in my teens, as far as I could remember, the feeling that one is going to lose one's youth in the future, and the mountains of time ahead... But enough of these contemplations, to get on with my story, or rather, Our Adventure Book! As I lay on my bunk, resting from my days of journeying by sea and land, I could hear the giggles of females coming from the Couples Room, perhaps, reminiscent of the buildings past history. The dormitory was packed full with kipping bodies everywhere, piles of rucksacks, with the din of street activity, and the hot-air, as if some huge fan were blowing it through the high-ceiling rooms of the once Turkish Prison. I pondered, but my only sure thought was to get some sleep, and then, to get on the road South, away from town-life, over the mountains to find a better way!...

After some sleep I felt better and decided to go and sample some Souvlakis, a small Pitta and Kebab with a yogurt sauce, and have some more wine to make me sleep again. Finding a small tavern I sat down and ordered. I would visit this place many times in the future

9

but now all was fresh and new, and I would never experience it so again. The wine came first, and relaxed my travelling-nerves, as I watched the innkeepers two baby daughters charcoal the meat and heat the pitta-bread. They were about ten years old, dark-haired, and a bit precocious; learning Cretan adult-ways. The landlord had been a seaman and travelled the world and now he was a happily-married man; which seemed to me then as now, to be the perfect state to be in! This bustling Town was full of passageways, interesting shops and workshops of all sorts, to get lost in. Once you got away from the tourist traps, there was plenty of adventure to be had, such as the Icon Painters Studio; the local cafes and meeting places, the tourist-shops full of fertility statuettes, linked somehow with the Cretan past. These erotic figureens standing side by side with the beautiful Icons of the Madonna and Saints. The Cretan sense of irony! A thousand other connotations rattled in my head; Greek Mythological History, the monkeys in the Minoan murals in Athens, Yeats-Byzantium. The Gods and Goddesses of Mythological Times; the black and blue colours or Crete and the Ireland I had left behind me a long time ago!

What was it to do with the Modern European way, I was trying to escape from? How would I find the "Good Place" (I didn't know yet that it really existed somewhere over the Hills). The Mystery blurred in my mind as I made my way along the seafront in search of a bar.

I wandered into a place of the Hippy Era. Weird and Surreal Paintings covered the walls of this large, long bar; it was somehow cosy but dark and introspective in mood. Sliding doors separated it from another long Bar at the rear, where the old men played cards and discussed, what, I did not know. Past a huge mirror and a big picture of Bogart, the end of the bar led out into another street. The landlord was a big, friendly man and served me a bottle of Retsina with a smile. He looked like a man who had helped many people in trouble. The music was definitely the 'Doors', as if the place was caught in Time! The end of the bar I sat in, faced the Seafront which had a borderline of palm trees; which suggested to me huge carrots, then pineapples, giving the place a Cuban look. When, as a raw traveller, the imagination is stirred and one tries to fit things in to place. I viewed the holiday makers strolling along the strand.

At each restaurant, waiters canvassed for customers, almost grab

10

bing their victims. In terms of fashion this big bar was ten years out of date, but nevertheless, interesting, and would someday disappear with a new tourist trade. It was amusing in my present fluid situation, but I could do this anywhere; so I just watched the warm evening closing in and then moved to another bar. The music and drinking places were opening up. The Front was lined with hundreds of tables and chairs, which were slowly filling up with people enjoying themselves. I sat and watched for a time the many beautiful women reconnoitre an evenings entertainment. The sun was sliding down below the Ocean and a cool breeze was blowing. Despite the crowds of holiday-makers, the place was regaining its romance and Venetian beauty. By the fruit-gardens, couples dallied and along the Tavernas of the Venetian Port dinners were being served and there was the smell of freshly caught fish being cooked. I went to a bar and sat at a table looking for conversation and listening to music; somewhat lonely I must admit, while I dreamt dreams of Crete - which were only beginning to formulate themselves in my head. With some wine at this time of day, the imagination seems to play tricks, but is eased by good company or a sweetheart: then anything seems possible! There was a group of mixed company I joined somehow, and a conversation, that I cannot now remember, ensued.

"Dream Talks". Winter.

The Discovery

For some unknown reason I decided to get off the bus on a corner on the top of some hills. The road straight ahead, wound its way down the valley to the sea. To the right of me, a road went up, around, and across the hills.Strangely, nobody else alighted from the bus, which was now disappearing into the Olive Groves. I walked up the road, carrying my load, not yet aware, on this lovely Summer's afternoon that a new leaf of my life, was about to be turned over. After some time walking, I came around a treelined corner, the olive trees still wrapped and the black nets tied with rope, waiting for the olives to ripen. Then the nets would be placed on the ground to catch the oily fruit. A dog barked in the distance, and an old man walked past me, head bowed, eyes to the ground. There was a village up there! (to my surprise) ahead of me. I could see a white church with a cross; the village-clock was stopped at quarter-to-two, and there was nobody else about. To the right of me was a long white-washed Taverna, with three doors, and a German lager sign; a shop to the left of me, beyond which were a few scattered chairs, (as if people had been sitting there, and had suddenly left) on the raised balcony-like side of the road. This overlooked the most beautiful view I had ever seen in my life! But at the same time, it seemed to be familiar to me in some mysterious way! Was this the Peninsula, jutting out into the blue green sea, I had painted in my imagination, as a young boy in Ireland? And there were two Peninsulas out there! one to the left, one to the right! I stopped for a moment and gazed at my dream come true. Thirsty, I laid my baggage near some tables and chairs outside the Taverna. I ventured for some cool shade. Inside, there were rows of tables and chairs, recently cleaned and tidied; and by some stroke of luck, there were paintings of the Modern kind, on the walls. In front of me, was a bar with a swing door; with lines of bank-notes of different countries pinned to the bottle-filled shelves: of everything from Ouzo to Scotch Whisky. In the middle of the display was an Irish punt with an illustration from the Book of Kells. Near the bar was an entrance to the kitchen. And I didn't even notice (in my amazement) that sitting at a desk, in the corner by the door was a black-moustached man in his 20's; writing and using a calculator. He was black-shirted, and tall: I could tell by the way he sat stooped. He gave me a routine disinterested look, and said "Conas a ta tu?" in a language, I only knew a few words of. "Ta me go mait" I answered. Not really realizing what I was saying.

Then a flood of half-remembered foreign words hit my consciousness.

Then he smiled and said in English;

"Would you like something to drink?"

"A big beera" I replied in a relieved manner. He went behind the bar and handpumped out the beer, and so became a bit more friendly. At that precise moment, I felt as if I had returned home at last, after years of wandering. It was the most pleasant time of the day for that time of day that I had ever experienced; as there I sat on a high stool at the bar with a happy day outside, and a cool breeze blowing.

"You change cheques?" I said.

"Yes," he said, seriously. "Passport!"

I handed him my green passport. He glanced at it, and his face broke and almost cracked with a grinning smile.

"Mr Irishman!"

First Meetings in Stavros

I remember climbing up the stone steps to the hostel, seeing the balcony for the first time, the plants on the wall, with Granny watering them, the washing-line, the shaving mirrors and the spiral staircase, which led to the roof-bunkrooms. I remember the Irish writer sitting at the office-desk; how, I gave him my green passport with the Harp on it. I said "Sorry, it's Irish!" "There's no problem with that here!" he responded, with an intelligent tone. I carried my rucksack up the metal stairway to find a bunk, had a short sleep and then went down to the bar, and talked to the tall black-haired black-moustached man. "Another Irishman" he said, with a friendly smile. "Would you be after' a beer?" asked the writer; "My name's Pat" he slipped in as he shook my hand.

"Indeed, I would. I've got a terrible thirst!" I replied (with a semi-affected Irish accent). We sat at one of the long tables with two bottles of beer and he offered me one of those Greek cigarettes. I felt like a child in new wonderful surroundings, timid and tired, but keen to satisfy my longing for friendship and well-being. I had been through a lot of bad times, and I knew, nervous though I was still, that the good-times were about to begin! I was glad to be speaking to a fellow countryman, even though as a matter of fact he had come direct from our island and given England a miss, where as I had been away for twenty years! I was also happy to be speaking Irish-English, my natural foreign tongue and not struggling with the formal complications of the Queen's English. We drank a few beers with pleasure and with art; I calmed down and got into the conversation, commonly referred to as the Crack! We talked about Art and life and drank slowly, in a refined manner. My first impressions of the place were lucid and sensitive. We both knew that we had come upon a good-thing and knew that we were appreciating it; others would not even see. Why want anything else! I enjoyed the experience of such new faces and fresh feelings. About 7 o'clock, I did my first pencil drawing; of Popa, half-asleep with his friends in the Taverna. This, my first drawing in Stavros, was scribble like in style, but had all the right ingredients for a painter, of

The Peninsula.

which I cannot relate in words. I had, due to the total unexpectedness of the situation, only pencils and sketchbooks. So I had to draw. But next time, I would return with ample brushes and paints! Pat said later to Nikos, "Brendan is an Artist, and he wants to come back here in January to paint!" This was Pats way of setting me up for the Youth-Hostel-Managers job! He had been here a year and wanted to go back to Kerry to see his mother. For now, I would draw, draw, draw! Besides the marvellous faces and characters in the Taverna, Moma, Granny, Popa, Nikos and the local villagers, there was the landscape and the seascape, olive-groves and the black-nets! The colour was out of this world. That evening, Moma laughed, as she said something to Nikos, pointing to Pat and me standing in the door-way of the taverna, staring out at the red sun dropping behind the Cape. Pat and I were saying in unison "It's gone, it's gone!"

In the next century-long, two weeks, I would meet, as well as the locals, many other interesting travellers and foreigners, and explore the local area with an American word-processing woman. I said to her "Would you like to come for a walk?" We strolled up the road to Sellia. It was a winding road, with many ravines, and of course, I was, at that time, a complete coward! So I walked on the inside of her. I had that Irish way of walking, (Ponder, dear reader, the Earths axis!) which I learnt from my brother; i.e: one always walked at an angle towards your fellow-walker, gradually pushing them off to the left! Once, she nearly went over the side! She remarked later to Pat-the writer "Today, what do you think? This man nearly pushed me over the cliff!" We returned to the hostel (She wasn't used to walking long distances) and I saw walking, not only as exercise, but also as an Art-form. She was pretty and plump, with fine long brown-hair. She was a bit of a psychologist, very clever and fascinating to talk to. Francis, Pat and I would have interesting triangular conversations and she liked Anais Nin the diarist. At the time, I detested that kind of stuff and so I used to rile her for fun quoting Mr Norman Mailer whom I admired, especially, his writings on the existential repercussions of Technology-Land; which was what I was running away from! As were many other travellers! They didn't want videos and discos, but rather, village conversation and live-action, away from the fantasies of Technology. Francis made a lot of money from computers and regretfully, I never said No! when she offered me anything, and I was envious of her wad of credit cards. One day, (I thought) in the future,

Popa half-asleep with his friends in the taverna.

A Five mile walk around Selia.

would we have to go even further away than Stavros? or was there really no escape! For now, it didn't matter. I was soaked in an excellent way of life, and all that was really missing was a sweetheart! Francis was my good friend, though Nikos assumed that we were lovers! Sometimes, a tall English decorator would join us on our walks, and sometimes the group would swell to seven. We would walk to Lefkoyia for a drink or to anywhere that took our inclination. And it was the best of times.

For about a week, Francis and I would go on long walks; every day we would set off in a different direction. Now and then, we would sleep under the stars in our sleeping bags, side by side, like brother and sister. Sometimes, I would kiss her goodnight, but that was as far as it went. One day, we had walked from Plakias, along by the Cape; wandering along a cliff-path, which made its way, eventually, to Damnoni Beach. It was late in the year for holidaymakers, and there was a lone-woman, fishing, throwing a line out into the sea. She wore a blue bandanna, and she had her hair cut like Ava Gardner in the film Night of the Iguana. Francis admired the womans apparent independence. The weather was hot and the sea warm. We strolled along the beach and breathed the sea air; the waters here were not so salty; so the air was sweet. Past Damnoni, we walked, up the cliff path near the caves, below which was a sheltered cove, called Nudist-Beach, where several naked people were sunbathing and swimming; as we made our way past this place, a naked man crossed our path and was very close and then a nude woman. The sight of pubic hair and other attachments was not embarrassing, but rather perplexing: since we were fully clad and bearing heavy rucksacks. We carried on, along the rocky deserted hills and cliffs, until eventually, we reached, what turned out to be Paradise Beach! We came around some rocks, to face a hotel with holiday rooms and a big, blue, private swimming pool. In the distance, was a beautiful sheltered bay. We made our way to the beach and I immediately went for a swim. The sea was a blue-green and was my idea of a Pacific-island, a castaway cove. The water was clear, with the sunlight spotlighting the seaweeds and fish. (Francis said that evening, that we were the wrong partners in the right place!) Anyway, back in the U.S. she had two boyfriends! She had meant of course, that if we had been sweethearts, the whole situation would have been perfect! And I admitted to her that, being human, I needed a girlfriend, both romatically and physically. I often felt like a centaur on heat, but there wasn't enough time to care and plenty to interest me. The night closed in and the vast sky was full of stars and the light from the full moon. We laid our bags on dry sand by some sloping rocks. It was getting chilly, I collected some briers and driftwood, set up a stone grate and lit a fire. Francis was taken aback by my ingenuity, and said, in a slightly ambiguous joking way "Amazing! How did you do it? Where did you get the firewood from?" I said "It was easy. We used to do this when I was a kid!" Have people forgotten everything! "You see, it's usual in Art schools, and Artists have always been doing so." They put you in an Art School Studio, with bits and pieces of various material and say - Now, make something! And so, you basically, use what is available! And the Cretans do it all the time, because they cannot always afford or get hold of the things they need; nails, machines etc. Maximum use of minimum means! The result can look a bit Heath-Robinson in material and construction, but they work! Francis was good on human psychology, but, like a lot of her contemporaries, lacked an awareness of subjects outside her own speciality! Amazing, the permutations and tangents one goes off on, from just building a fire! But really! it was one of the most beautiful of evenings, and nothing else mattered! The next day, on our way back, I said "I know, a shortcut to Plakias". It was about one hour to nightfall and she followed me.

Unfortunately, I was wrong and we got lost in the twighlight among the prickly pears and bracken. Eventually, we found our way again. She was small and heavy, and had to climb over a barbed-wire fence.

She ripped her blue-jeans, and was steaming with anger; I giggled and restrained a laugh and she yelled at me, for my incompetence! I had never seen her angry before and I was surprised at a usually calm psychologist showing her emotions! Down along the beach we walked, silently. The place was deserted with a wind coming up. Winter was coming, though to us, it was mostly like an English Summer! there along the pebby beach of Plakias. The sand was gusting up on our clothes and getting in our hair; and I felt like a good drink! The bars were closing and we walked towards Plakias, the beach trees bending with the wind and the umbrella clad tables were abandoned by the remaining holiday-makers. The bakery and grocery shop were shut and some villagers and backpackers were waiting for the last bus; which stopped at Stavros, on its way to Rethymnon. Michealangelo and some of his mates were having a beer inside the cafe by the bus-stop. Nikos's white van was parked outside. We past by, like total strangers, with the village faces gawking at any slight change of circumstance. When the madding winds came up from Africa; the tourists would leave partly because of the sand blowing on the beach; and in the winter, Cretan life would start to dominate again. It was a time for closing-ranks, and telling-stories and finding a wife. Only the travellers and writers, expatriates and exiles, would stay; but the feeling was everything is closing down; I felt homesick, but for where, I didn't really know! It was in this mood that I entered the Fish restaurant. Francis was putting off going back to America and I didn't want to go back to England at all. Moma Plakias was sitting squarelegged peeling some vegetables and her sons were serving the few customers. Some soft popular Greek music was the only thing in the background. Jim, the decorator arrived; an English couple who kept cudding each other and then the Canadian Indian joined us.

Two French students came across from some tables in the far corner, and we all joined three tables together, Last-Supper-fashion, and ordered a fish meal, beer and wine. My sardine-like fish when served had small bullet-like holes and sharpenelled heads. Sometimes, one would hear explosions coming from the sea. Dynamite was a sure bait! I remembered on the island of Paros, seeing a couple of men with missing arms and legs. I thought that it was the War, but apparently, it was only the fishing. Outside on the Sea, some boats were fishing, before it got really rough. Once, Michaelangelo had been out there in a big storm with a couple of young fishermen. One of them started to cry tears for his Mother. Michaelangelo stood up in the boat, storm waves heaving, and all of them close to death' and slapped the crying man, saying, in his usual vehement, almost histrionic, bravadoish way - "If your going to die, die like a man!" The man was more frightened of Michaelangelo than he was of the storm! and shut up. They survived to tell the tale.

We were enjoying our dinner and finishing off the wine, when suddenly, the Taverna door burst open. A freezing wind gushing in and lifting the tableclothes. An empty beer-bottle fell off the table and rolled on the floor. We all stopped, mid-sipping and munching, and looked up at a thin teenage man, dressed only in a teeshirt and shorts; with sandled bare feet, short fair wet-hair, redfaced, with cuts and bruises on his arms and legs, and drenched to the skin! He entered in a determined manner looking perturbed, and despite his skinny build, he was obviously a courageous and virile person. He had a small walking bag on his back; and he immediately sat down at the head of the table, (one elbow and hand in saintly gesture) and said, in a fraught but not desperate way; with a Parisian accent - "I must have a drink!" As he poured and gulped-back a glass of strong wine, he added with the immediacy of an Ancient Greek messenger at the death's door, "I must tell someone! what I have just been through!!!" We all stopped to listen!

"A couple of days ago I felt compelled to hike down the Samaria Gorge, but on arrival at Hania, I discovered that it was closed for the Winter! ... so I made my way back by bus to Plakias. Then I decided to approach and reach the Gorge, by walking along the coast; I walked much of the way, but I also managed to get some short lifts. Bypassing the beautiful Frangokastello, I eventually came upon Anopoli, a quiet small country town; the birth place of the Cretan Rebel leader, Dhastkaloyiannis. Two days later, inside a Taverna for a beer, I crossed paths with a distressed fellow-countryman of mine, also from Paris. He was sitting drinking a brandy, wearing only swimming-trunks! He was marked from head to toe with cuts and bruises; as I was partly so, myself; with the added discomfort of raw palms!

He told me the most amazing tale! He too had an uncontrollable desire to walk down the Samaria Gorge; and knowing that it was dangerous and closed for the Winter months, he nevertheless made the trip! ("We all were spellbound, as he paused for a moment to drink some wine, I offered him a cigarette, but he didn't smoke; the wind was howling outside, but it was shamelessly comfortable inside!) The Parisian continued - "He succeeded in completing the hazardous journey with the added handicap of a heavy rucksack, which contained all of his belongings. On reaching Ayia Roumeli, he was shocked to find that there were no boats until the following March!... He was disinclined to make the walk along the coastal footpath at this time of year, but being a strong long-distance swimmer, he decided to swim from Ayia Roumeli to Loutro!" We couldn't believe our ears! and I lit another Greek cigarette, with anticipation. On the face of it, it was a short swim for a seasoned swimmer; so he stripped down to his trunks; and left his rucksack behind-hidden in some rocks. He carefully parceled his Passport and money into a plastic-bag and tied it

The sea barrage at Rethymnon-like sugar lumps.

around his neck!... He did manage to swim from Ayia Roumeli to Loutro!... The Parisian paused again, as if he were drained of energy, and I prompted him - "How, how did he do it???..."

"Well, my friends, instead of the two hours he expected to swim, it took him 7 hours! It would have been easy, he thought, to shadow the coast, but sadly, the sea was rough, and so he was continuously dashed and smacked against the rocks. He was covered in cuts..." Francis broke in - Oh My God! How horrible! Jim asked - What happened then? The Parisian turned to Jim, with a smile - This is the funny part! When he at last got to Loutro, he crawled and staggered up out of the stormy sea, covered in blood! and in a state of exhaustion and confusion... whereupon, the villagers saw him. They screeched in Greek "Where has he come from, this man?" They ran to him and pulled him out. At first they thought that he was a ghost or shipwrecked sailor. When he told them his story; they roared with laughter, at the crazy tourist.

We sat at the table and thought that was the end of the story, and stopped for drink and smoke - Francis looked at me and said "Wow"! Then, to our surprise, the Indian teacher interruped - "Listen!" as she poured the Parisian another glass of wine, "There is more!" We all paid attention! The Parisian continued... "You see", he said "I too was physically wrecked when I met him! I had the day before climbed up and over the 2453 metres high mountain range, without any climbing gear, and down the other side to the Gorge! I was frightened to death, more scared than I have ever been in my whole life, and then, I had to climb all the way back again!" All of us were transfixed by his tale. The Parisian looked so weak to take such crazy risks. He didn't appear to be foolish in any way, but like many inexperienced travellers, probably hadn't thought about it and let everything happen to him! In

23

foreign countries, the stranger can easily get into trouble of all sorts - with his misconceptions!

I asked him - "What did you do then?"

"I was completely fucked!"... he paused, as if there was no more to tell!... then, he said casually..." The swimmer asked me to help him!" What more could happen? I surmised as I looked at Francis' lovely girlish hair. "He had left all his belongings on the other side of the mountain-range in the Village of Ayia Roumeli and he pleaded with me to help him!" Jim., the decorator asked the Parisian - "What did you do?"... "We went all the way back over the mountain, and we came back again with his gear!"

The Parisian had concluded his story, and so I asked him, making polite conversation - "What do you do for a living in Paris?" He replied, in a well mannered way "Oh, I'm a Steeplejack,".

"And what will you do now? I enquired.

"Well, I have no money left, so I'll go and work on the Olive-Harvest"

"You need some clothes. It's getting cold!"

"Ah, these will do!" he replied, looking at his clothes.

After, another gulp of wine, he left and disappeared out into the chilly seaswept night.

Francis, Jim and I, would, once a week or so, go into Rete by bus for shopping, drinking and changing our travellers-cheques. We would stay at the Rethymnon Hotel, and in the evening go to the "Hippy Bar" on the seafront. I was always scared on the bus - when we went around those narrow bends in the road, with small-barriers and sheer ravines. Of course, there was little to worry about; the school-children made the same journey every day. But when I saw the blackly dressed women making the Sign-of-the-Cross, when the bus passed the many small shrines by the road, my stomach dropped. Were these shrines for all those who had gone over the side? On one particular day, the driver had asked all the passengers to move to the front of the bus because the back-wheels were over the side! Usually, the bus wobbled a bit, as there were stacks of rucksacks piled high on the roof-rack and the buses were sometimes overcrowded. But the ever-present danger of the journey made arrival at each destination more exciting, and also worked up my thirst!

At the Rete hostel, a party of French school delinquents, set fire to some of the hostel beds, and the fire-brigade was called. When they arrived, the fire was out and so they fined the hostel lady many thousands of drachmas. She was sitting at her desk crying. Previously, at the Stavros hostel, they had broken open the water-mains and flooded Nikos's-Taverna. Nikos used to say "You get all kinds of rubbish passing through here!" Francis would buy presents for her family and friends; and later we would take Souvlakis and beer and listen to cheerful Greek music and get right back into the atmosphere of Crete. While she shopped, I would investigate the various kinds of Fertility-Statuettes; depicting newly married couples on beds, with giant phalluses and breasts. These were, I believe, given as wedding-gifts. There were also the demigods with erect-parts, which I had also seen on postcards; and I wondered if they had any connection with the Ancients? (Or with my own carnal desires). On one such trip (with the hope of satisfying my wishes), I went in search of condoms; I found a Chemist and asked in English. But the Chemist did not understand - so I drew the shape of a large condom with my pencil. He understood immediately and said "Oh, yes, yes, yes".

When I later looked at the contraceptives, they were extra-large! just as was Cretan self- esteem.

In the cool of the evening, the three of us would sit outside the "Hippy Bar", talk and watch the passers by. The huge palm-trees, would give the place a South-America foreground and add to the undoubted charm of the town. Sometimes we would meet interesting travellers and at other times, we would see foreign deadenders lounging in the bar, sipping cheap Retsina. It was the kind of scene I wished to avoid, not so much the drinking, but the boredom...! The landlord was kindly, and always presented a new customer with a free bottle of wine - as a welcoming present.

But after a few days, it was a joy to return home to Stavros. On the way back, an old lady in black said to me "Are you from Stavros?" So I was fitting in and not merely a tourist! I always suspected, despite the beauty of the place and the character of the people, many of my assumptions and allusions were incorrect, though some weren't. I

"Fertility statuette"

was sure that Greece was friendly and unreserved and that the sun shone, but I could see many of the Tourists and Travellers mistaking ordinary conversation and events , for things extraordinary. As if they had never heard before; "How goes it?", "Okay mate?" In a way everywhere and everybody, is in essence the same! A week later, Francis and I would be making the three-day bus ride to London, from sun, into the snow of Switzerland, then to cold, grey England. It was rough going to Athens by Coach, but at least it was an experience in which we were, slowly, approaching the sun! But going back to the greyness and cold of Britain (in more ways than one) was hellish! Better to fly back!

On our return journey to London, we had just crossed the Border from Yugoslavia into Italy and it was raining cats and dogs, with the bus-lights beaming into the spray, which flowed down the windows. We were halfdead and in a drowsy semi-sleep, and cramped together in the uncomfortable bus-seat. (In Belgium the buses change over to a modern bus, with videos etc, from a grotty, 2nd World-War coach, so that only the journey between London and Belgium was comfortable, (So beware Traveller!). Anything could happen; a wheel came off on the Autobahn and the driver asked us to move to one side, we were left in the Swiss Alps for 2 days etc, of the bus, etc. But now and then something really funny happened!

From this London-bound bus, we heard some commotion coming from the driver's seat (sometimes, the drivers would change without stopping the bus, by climbing over each other!) and then the bus came to a sudden halt. We looked, to see a man carrying two large suitcases. He was soaked to the skin, and dressed all in white! a ghostly fi-

Fertility Statuette at Rethymnon.

Fertility statuelle at Rethymnon.

gure and on his head, he wore a Chefs-hat! The kindly and curious Greek drivers had stopped in pity and let this strange hitch-hiker on to the overcrowded bus (some extra passengers were sleeping in the aisles). We were all curious as to what he was doing in such unusual attire and circumstances? He spoke Arabic! but luckily, an Arab-student traveller translated...

This Arabic Chef worked in Milan, and needing his teeth filled, had hitch hiked down to Yugoslavia, where treatment was free. (There used to be a big sign at the Border-Post, which said in no uncertain terms - Free Health Service...). Guessing what the Chef was after (He also had no Passport), the Yugoslavian Police had turfed him back into Italy... Now, on the bus back to Stavros, London was far from my mind; and I was looking forward to seeing new faces and new friends. There had been a sunshower, but soon the outbreak had cleared; the sun was shining and a full rainbow could be seen clearly in the valley below Sellia.

When I was not with Francis, I would go sketching and draw the Olivetrees and black nets, but on this trip, I would not go into great depth; making quick studies and cartoons of the place. There wasn't enough time to do large canvasses and I didn't have the right art-materials, or cash to buy them. But a lot can come out of those spontaneous impressions, one first gets of a place and the people. It's all new and wonderous.

Once, I was strolling in the streets around Plakias, when I accidently came upon the Greek widow's shop, which sold paintings. I found the entrance in a small secluded courtyard, from which there was a good view of the sea. On an easel was perched a small oil-painting of Plakias Bay and the Cape. It was competent, but not exactly to my taste. The place was deserted, so I ventured into the dimly lit shop. It was full of handmade jewllery and pottery and finely embroidered silk and Greek dresses. As I turned around to leave, I was surprised by a petite female figure in the doorway; the woman, about thirty, had long black hair, almost Japanese! in the intensity of its dark hue. She was smiling and radient, and she wore a slightly long dress, embellished with light-reflecting tinsel needlework. On her arms were bangles, on her ears were small jewelled earings and on her feet, sandals. She had a full womanly figure, and a mature demure, poise. I stared at her for some time, as I would at a Hindu woman, showing no infor-

Wrapped Olive Trees.

◄ *Olive Trees and Nets* ▼

malities or signs of desire. She waited for me to speak and I for her. "Do you need anything?" she asked me, in a respectful voice. "No" I replied, shyly, as I made haste past her. As I came out of the door, she must have turned, as I did myself, to get a glimpse of her face in the light. The face was soft, with fine amber eyes and full lips. She lowered her eyes, as I looked directly into them! until her eyelids almost closed shut. I turned around to go, and then she said softly, but precisely, "Come again, won't you!" I answered most certainly, "Yes, I will!" and walked away, smiling to myself.

On my return to the Taverna, in the late of the evening, I found Pat and Francis playing cards. I got a beer from the bar and joined them. When Pat went ouside to the toilet, Francis inquired of me, in a whispering voice - "Where did you go this afternoon? I was looking for you everywhere." "Oh, I went to visit the Greek widow!" I said, seriously, though full of Limerick blarney. "Just the kind of rich woman that you need, and in the right place" she smiled. "Yes" I said, knowing I had hit on something rare.

Pat came back and we played cards. Once, I made secret signs to him in Irish, so we could cheat, but my attempts at cheating were embarrassing, because I couldn't really speak my mother tongue, and had to make do with a foreign one. Never mind learning Cretan or Greek, I had attended a model school where English was taught as a foreign-language and so, when I came to England, I would hardly write my name in the language of that country. As for my time at the Christian Brothers, where the living daylights were beaten out of us, this would crop up in later conversations, in Nikos's Taverna. For now, my head was pre-occupied with the black-haired widow, and the softness of her olive skin! She had touched my heart and I knew I would visit her many times more! The young English businessman, joined our card playing company, as did a few hikers. He was my namesake, but he wasn't burdened with my finances or apparent humility. Nikos didn't care for him. It was said that he had bought women, including Francis. This I couldn't believe at all! Anyway, he wore his jacket over his shoulders, one sleeve off, like a hussar, and this manner of dress gave him a pompous look. But, on one of my later visits, his reputation had improved and he was getting on well, or maybe, business was bad. Still, you never can tell! Outside, in the road, we could hear the voice of the Donkey-Woman (she was nicknamed so, because hers was the loudest in the village, and certainly, the loudest voice I had ever heard in my life!) Her husband, after years, and nearly deaf, had done a bunk to Athens! She was screaming, at the top of her echoing voices - "Jonnie, come in for your tea, won't you. Where are you Jonnie? Where are you? Come in, come in. Wait till I get my hands on you. Wait until your father gets home!" Other women, of more refined natures, were replying "Shut up, you old dog!" One said to me, out in the street - "How would you like her between your sheets?" Moma laughed; Nikos laughed, we all laughed! Men, women and children wandered up and down the street, gossiping and talking and doing their business. It was early evening, and the men were coming in for a drink, after rising early and a long day. The women were cooking and the priest was sharing a drink with Popa, the Wee-Man, who was dressed in black, Cretan style, and two men from somewhere else. Of course, when the tourists saw all these people sitting around in the late afternoon, they assumed that the Greeks did nothing else! Moma would work from dawn to dusk; cook in the Taverna, and then in the evening, go home and do her own housework. And she would laugh at us - holiday children! And, in the summer season, Nikos could never leave the business for long. Still, I loved it all, and could only go away from this, my home, in the knowledge, that I would one day return, arrive again, after a long journey and absence, walk in and say "Hello" and sit at the bar. Nikos would give me a welcome drink, and I would smile and live again; look out at the view, and in at the people and know I had arrived at the best place. For the present, for me, this was the new-found-out.

Francis and I used to sit in Nikos's Taverna, above the Bay of Plakias, which was visited by various travellers (young and old). Some would stay in Nikos's others, in Plakias hostel, just outside the 'town'. There was a different kind of atmosphere and different kinds of people staying in that hostel. It depended on what kind of interest you had. We preferred Nikos's, where eventually you would meet everybody, at some time. There was a good mixture of locals and foreigners, and the mood of the place had always something new to offer. Often, it would be quiet and mellow, to the point of sleepiness, and it could change unexpectedly, with a new influx of visitors; other times, it would be unbearably busy and noisy, so we would leave, or sit outside. The locals seemed to like it also, and they would come from, as far away as Lefkoyia village. We would compare notes on foreign travellers, who held a particular interest for us, and particular-

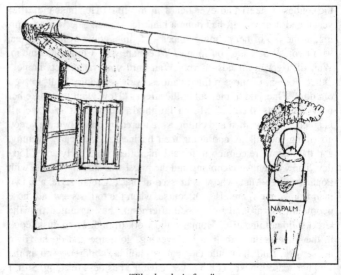

"The kettle is free".

ly, the mysterious, private, attractive and reserved people who just ate in the taverna and didn't get involved. Often, they turned out to be couples in love or having secret affairs, writers, artists. Maybe we would take an interest in people because of their unusual or outstanding looks, or clothes, and we would try to guess, what they were all about. One particular couple grabbed our attention straight away. They were both dressed in glossy black leather biking gear. The man was in his forties, slim, with a thin moustache and a small pointed beard. He had medium-long brown hair and generally, a musketeer like appearance, but he was unapproachable; he definitely wanted to be left alone with his female companion. This couple were friendly only to the point of nice smiles. She was extraordinarily beautiful, Dutch and tall with short brown hair, and in the white walled taverna, with its background of paintings and dark haired Greeks, she looked all the more so. They never remained long. They were staying in one of the Villages in a rented flat. Francis guessed her to be a model and I agreed, but later it turned out that she was an artist, like myself, and he was a Psychotherapist in Amsterdam. They had sold up to travel and they were now biking to Egypt. (She reminded me of Sylvia Krystel, the film-star).

34

In that first week in Stavros, my senses were rejuvinating themselves, after a long dull period in England, and so I was open to beauty. My feelings and perceptions were heightened, not with any kind of drug, but with the sheer beauty and reality of things; just as an artist should be. There was nothing to clutter up my life; all I needed was a minimum of possessions, good health and a little cash, so it was easy to experience the basics of life. I could get to know people in a very short time, make friends or enemies, and get to know myself and come to grips with things. Looking at the Dutch woman's face was like looking at a painting, because here, we were in a painting! We could all afford the sensibilities of artists and Pat the writer knew this. He'd say "We are artists. We understand". Some people who visited the village, didn't want to leave at all, and they would cry on the morning of departure; others, would gain or lose nothing! And after a long time in the village, one could reach what A. Milne would call (he was retired with his wife and painting was now his hobby) - "Saturation Point" - the kind of opposite of boredom. Drenched in colour, faces, sun, conversations, music; after regaining my sense of taste and smell, and clearing my head of all the rubbish of the media, and consumer nonsense, it was refreshing to the point to fatigue! At the time, I didn't bother to analyse things too much, but rather, tasted everything at hand, and met the people, an Alaskan miner, a Red-Indian-Canadian teacher, a student from Iceland, two Japanese cyclists; two friendly Swedish Television photographers, looking for film-material, an English hippy, a thousand others. There were many, many, tourist stories. Nikos said "You could write a book about all the people who have come through here!"

There was the Italian Artists model, petite, a Neopolitan with short jet black hair. I had just met her. Pat made a pass and had a fight with her. The next morning she was gone forever. Then, there was the two guys, on a bike story: They were travelling to Egypt on the same bike! and they had met in a funny way! This mad, hairy, bearded young-man was hitch-hiking in Italy, on his way to the Greek Islands, when a bike stopped. "Where are you going?" asked the hitcher; "To Egypt!" replied the biker, followed by, "Well, get on then!"... And he never got off!!

Then there was the French-Canadian student I liked to talk to. He wore a college scarf and looked like Jerry Lewis in the "Nutty Professor". We would try and invent new Newspeak Words - as in Orwells 1984 - and have intellectual conversations about various topics. He could be very argumentative, if that means anything, and he was very egocentric. Francis said, that there were few people she had met on her years travelling trip, who had the ability to listen to other people! Most were just talking about themselves! Then there were the two young Irishmen, who spent two hours getting absolutely drunk. One was quiet and the other, was riotous, calling Nikos "A Fecken Arab". Nikos promptly kicked him bumwise, into the road, before he knew what hit him, and he immediately came back again and again for more, until his friend dragged him away. Nikos was easy on the fellow, because he knew it was only the mans character and the drink! I whispered to the quiet Irishman "be careful Sean, they're all armed here! Get your mate out of here before its too late!" This frightened the life out of him, and they went down the road, the drunk one shouting, "I'll get him, if it's the last thing I do!"

So there were many little stories and anecdotes to recount, on the long summer evenings... One morning I woke up, and got my towel and razor to shave. I passed the row of bunks outside on the roof. On one, a fifteen-year-old Dutch girl (I used to call her Lemon-Popscicle) was lying on a bare much-used mattress, spreadeagled, bare-breasted, wearing flowery panties. She was wriggling about and giggling. In one of the dormitories, there was another new arrival at the end of the trail, unpacking his rucksack. He was, I believe, in his late sixties, red-faced, nervous and tired. He had just come from Hydra, the artists island. In the evening, he sat in the taverna eating. He didn't speak much at first, but later he joined Cecile and me. A couple of days later, he went down the Samari Gorge and came back completely exhausted. But after that, he stayed for about a week. We didn't get to know him very well, and all we knew was, that he was retired and going to Africa. But on the day of his final departure, a strange thing took place. Cecile came up to me, in the taverna and said "You wouldn't mind to sign this, please?" I stared at the document, she had presented to me. It was an English Will. We both wondered if he was dying, and on the run! or whether he was merely being practical? A week later, he wrote to Cecile, thanking her for her kindness. I considered his fate in a serious way, but I could do nothing to change it,

and I had my own problems. But it did put things into perspective.

Out the door and over the wall.

Where is Maria?

"There's always someone worse off than yourself". I was tempted to utter that obnoxious saying, but anyway Ireland, the Treaty Stone, were now for me, ancient memories. The man with the Will left. He gave me an artists address in Hydra, and we never heard of him again. That was a constant aspect of this place - people came into and out of, my life with greater speed than is usually acceptable.

These theatrical entrances and exits could also be amusing and bi-zarre. One sunny afternoon, when most people were at the beach, I was enjoying one of Nikos's lemonades, and smoking a cigarette, looking at my morning's drawings. The only noise was the sound of the elec-tric fan. Nikos always came over, and made a comment, or criticism, but usually, we didn't speak much, in that period when he did his ac-counts. I had walked up the Donkey-path from Plakias to Stavros, and I had stinging, sweating, armpits. I was glad to be in the shade, out of the hot mid-day sun. I would get rainbows in my eyes from the bright light, and it was my favourite time for mixing. The paintings on the wall looked good, their colour was intense and the chiaroscuro was refined by the sunlight. (Soon, I would go onto the roof, and paint and sit.) I was sitting there alone, except for Nikos, when a bus-came into the village, came making a hell of a noise, doing a U-turn. Fifty pas-sengers rushed the taverna; (usually at the same time everyday), a party of Swedes packing the whole place, all eating ice cream, and Moma was rushed off her feet. This would all take about 20 minutes! Then, they would all be gone!

Within seconds, all would be still again; my mind would be full of olive nets, designs and compositions, cartoons, views and atmo-spheres of a serene nature, romance and tranquility. Then I would look out the taverna window at the view and the tables. Maybe some-one had arrived on the mid-day bus? Suddenly, a convoy of jeeps, with yelling tourists, would arrive, they would all buy a lemonade each, gulp it back, and speedily, with great commotion, chase off to invade the next village on their itinerary. Once, I put up an easel and started to paint, hoping some of them would buy one of my pictures, displayed by the wall, but no chance! When I was sitting there, paint-ing, wearing a Panama hat, I noticed a group approaching the village from the direction of Plakias. A lot of twelve blonde young Swedish girls and women were walking briskly up the road. They were grossly dressed and suntanned. They wore knee-length socks, leotards, as dancers at a rehearsal do. This was the latest Disco fashion, and it looked rediculously out of place and context. I couldn't believe my eyes. I almost cried with laughter! They, to my disappointment (I wanted to chat them up) passed Nikos's bound for the restaurant up the road - the Tapshop. I walked back into the taverna and said to serious Nikos "I've just seen the Disco-Swedes!" I went back outside again and looked out at the bay and the valley. An English 'Hippy' arrived, bought a bar of chocolate, and came over to me and said, pointing at the trees below in the valley, "Are they apple trees down there?" "What did you say?" I replied, as if I knew everything. Then, I said politely "Oh, I think that they are olive trees." Hippies had a bad reputation in the village because they lived so cheap, and that wasn't very good for business. Nikos and I made derogatory comments about the tourists who pleaded that they were being hard done by and overcharged, when really everything was so cheap and we were lucky to be here and enjoying such hospitaity. Some villages had been taken over by Hippies and so the locals couldn't make any cash. Eventually, the Lefkoyians would evict theirs. Otherwise the Hippies were doing no harm to anyone! The locals knew poverty and had had enough of it. They worked hard but didn't like to. They would go looking for work in the hope of not finding it! But there was a lot of building going on; half-finished, quarter-finished or to be finished in the off-season.

One morning, I woke up and looked down at Plakias. There was a new, relatively large wooden prefabricated building, where a few days previous, there had been nothing. "What is that?" I asked Cecile. "Its the new DISCO!" But this was on my second visit to Stavros, when some of the people I had met on my first visit, had vanished, or I had forgotten them; whereas, others, I could not rid from my mind and heart, so important were they to me!

Interlude

(Back in London I Brendan scribbled a fictional synopsis of his journey to Santorin.)

The Blue Bird

The play opens with Domenic, who works behind the scenes at the Blue Bird Opera House in Covent Garden, standing on the Tourist Deck of a large Greek passenger ship leaving Pireas Harbour, with the opening score from 'Indomeneo'. The Narrator describes the opera in synopsis; the frantic backstage scene changes in the opera's opening scene; and the boat journey: interior scenes and passenger activity. Domenic thinks of present events in Athens, the scenes around the Acropolis, the Eastern style Brothels in courtyards, the meat, fish and other markets. The riot in Athens Airport; in which Santorin-Islanders storm into the Airport office, shouting and screaming. They have been waiting for three days for their flights. The Official is desperately trying to explain, that the runway is dangerous because of rain. The airport guards, who shoot a mad seaman, after he has stabbed an innocent bystander. The Narrator describes scenes on various Aegean Islands at which the ship stops-on one island the tourist-Police Tower, looking like a watchtower, the drunken and First-World-War coated tramps on Paros. (Domenic in the Atlantis Hotel on Thera, from which he moonwatches in the early evening). "Strange that they are dressed like English dossers, the coats going down to the ankles in the burning sun".

On the voyage to Thera, Domenic is caught in a terrible storm, he dreams of the Trojan War, somehow mixed up with scenes from the Opera 'Indomeneo'. He promises to change his hedonistic ways, if he survives the storm. After arriving sick but safe in Paros, he meets a stranger, (his old self), in a taverna bar, with Greek pop-music in the background. As they converse, the Narrator cuts in with flashback scenes of the storm; in which the coaches below deck, break free from their moorings, and slide towards the shipside. This means certain disaster.

The passengers are all unaware of the danger, the seamen standby the lifeboats, but luckily the coaches are secured again. The ship is an ex-Mersey Ferry.

On Santorini, it is the feast of a Greek female Sea-Saint. Domenic, observes the long island procession, the scantily-clad, invisible tourists and the Greeks seem 'unaware' of their presence. That evening, when the whole of the island is candle lit by candles on church rooftops and in open doors, Domenic has a vision of a new life to come, his thoughts on the modern way contrast with this, its opposite?

The Peninsula jutting out into the green sea reminds him of the Sea-Monster in the opera, and he remembers his promise and knows that this will demand a sacrifice. He longs for love, and watches the aircraft land, near an Italian factory at Thera Airport. He reflects on the rubbish-heaps on the island beaches, and on the vast wastage of modern life. In a bar, Domenic meets Ed, who looks a bit like Chaplin. Later at a Dance, they meet Diana (Illia) and Celia (Electra). The latter can't wait to escape from the tourist islands. Domenic and Diana fall in love. He thinks how dark and mysterious she looks, and ponders on whether it is just a holiday romance, but their love developes amid holiday scenes.

On the beach, Dominic views the tourists bathing, and again, the rubbish heaps. A party of Islanders (with shotguns and gun belts) are hunting the Blue Bird (which is an island delicacy), come mysteriously up the beach. As they come closer to the sunbathers, who think that the hunters are intent on them for their nakedness, or that they are tourist haters? They raise their rifles and their arms move into an aiming position. The bathers dress frantically, as the hunters aim and fire. Some Blue Birds fall with a thumping sound to the ground. The tourists realize the reality of the situation and so undress again. Domenic feels a sense of great loss and guilt, knowing that he has seen victims die, he and Diana stroll along the sand, arm in arm.

Later in a taverna, a German Doctor speaks to Domenic and Diana about his part (he was not a Nazi, he emphasises) in the War on the Russian Front. Domenic reflects on his own lack of experience (as the German sips Atlantis wine).

Domenic and Diana sail away into the sunset; and slowly, as they look back at the Volcanic-island, Thera, Greek music blends back into the final score from "Indomeneo".

Part Two

Marianna

I sat painting the view of the bay; the two peninsulas, to the left and the right, stuck out into the green, torquoise sea, with some fishing boats coming in on the horizon. It was early afternoon on Crete and really too hot to paint, but I was trying! It was then that I saw Marianna for the first time. She came up on to the roof, by way of the spiral stairway - saw me and went into the sleeping rooms, came out again, and went down. Then, she came up again, walked over to me, looked at my watercolour, smiled a mad but friendly smile - made a comment! and then disappeared down the stairway again. She had long black hair, a well built sculptural frame with slightly broad breast-supporting shoulders. She smiled with large white teeth with a peculiar grimacing smile, which was really her only physical defect. She imagined herself (as I was to learn later) as a Tahitan, a flower-in-the-hair, grass-skirted South Sea islander. At this point in time, her manner was reserved, cautious and quiet and she was rarely seen in the Taverna, taking her meals upstairs and eating alone. But, Mama and the locals seemed to know her. Next time I met her I was under the shade of an Olive tree sketching. There she confided in me about her life and her problems. I liked her ways, though she tended to be child-like and potty, and she liked me. There was for me the kind of refreshment one gets from a satisfactory first meeting.

Anything she confided in me I would keep secret (I felt paternal towards her). But things began to get out of hand, once I let my defence down. She'd come in the Taverna as I sat quietly sipping ouzo on a tall stool at the bar, and laugh. Then she cried like a baby on my shoulder. At first, I didn't mind, as I was happy, and having the life of Reilly. I felt at home and she was the lost orphan, but later, her unpredictable behaviour was beginning to get on my nerves. Sometimes, when we were all seriously having dinner she would take off her blouse and giggle bare-breasted, or get under our table, sobbing and

43

Father Murphy outside Murphys Bar.

laughing. I tried to get her to draw. She had been to Art School in
Berlin, before she discovered the rewards of being a peepshow girl!
We drew each other, but she couldn't concentrate for long. She would
suddenly stop drawing, saying my drawing was architectural!, tear
hers up and laugh and then walk abruptly away.

I was treating the whole art business seriously. It was then that I
asked her to model for me down by the waterfall. Nikos, the Innkeeper, had asked me to paint him a nude for the Taverna, to put there
among all the other paintings, which were the background to our

The hostel and Taverna as a Stage Set.

Old Father Time approaching Mirthios.

"Dream Talks" on the long winter evenings. The next day, we set off down the hill through the olive groves and streams, past old men on donkeys, and women in vegetable plots to the waterfall, amid carmine flowers and bent trees. This river of small waterfalls, flowed between a gap in the olive groves that covered the hills, into a small glen. It was well vegetated and there were various types of wildlife; butterflies and insects of all kinds, hawks, crabs and herbs with all sorts of scents, bamboo trees, oleander bushes and prickly pear trees. The small river meandered its ways down the hillside past the old mill. She sat on the boulder with a red flower in her hair, moving most of the time, and asking me if she looked good with her hair this way, or that way. And I must admit, she had a beautiful figure, but I really did just want to draw her, mainly for the money Nikos had offered me, and to get involved with Marianna was asking for trouble, (Later a Dutch Adonis did, to his everlasting regret). Though if I hadn't thought about it, I probable would have. Mariannas parents were living apart. Her Greek mother in Berlin, her German father in Rodes. She said she was a Peepshow girl, and gave me a performance of her act. She was an incurable exhibitionist and at the slightest encouragement. She had a distraught childhood, and lots of Dollars from her extra services, (but I can't actually say whether I believed her or not). She claimed to be a virgin, except for an affair with a candle. She was about twenty six and wanted to be a secretary. She could type at speed and draw competently. She did what she did for the money. She was sincerely religious; and later when we walked past the Holy Grotto, she went into the Cave, knelt and prayed, as a devout Greek woman would. Reinoud, the Dutch Adonis, had an affair with Marianna. Eventually she would fly to Amsterdam to find him. She confessed to me, how one night he had seduced her. Despite her profession, Marianna was kind of innocent, and I felt sorry that it had happened. She fell in love with him, but he wasn't interested. He had enjoyed her body and that was all.

She said to me, in a boasting way, how he had taken her everyway, from the mouth, from behind, from the top and so on. She said, that he was her first lover, even though she worked in a Peep-show. Could I believe any of it? I don't know! For about a week, she chased him all the time, sometimes screaming and crying, until he had to leave! I remember him clearly, his curly, Bob Dylan hair. He was a man I found it easy to talk to.

View of Cape Kakomouri

The Irish writer and Cecile.
View of Cape Kakomouri.

Buying fruits

Walking to Lefkoyia.
Hostel Bunks

The Dutch - Girl Cecile.
The Road to Selia.

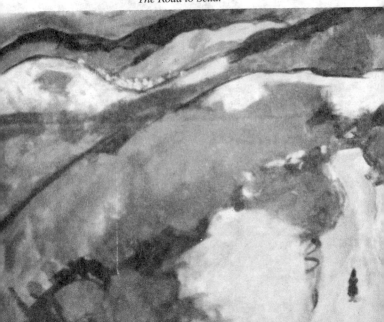

The Taverna
Nikos

Kissing at Damnoni.
The Taverna

The Dinner on the Roof

The moon is full and the table is set for dinner on the roof. Laid out are vegetable curry dishes, wine and fruits. A bit out of place having an Indian meal in Crete, but the dark-haired, gypsy-looking Aussi woman, had just arrived from that continent on her way to London, on the Australian Trek. She was almost raped by twelve men on a box-train, and jumped from the speeding wagon to safety. Soft music is coming from the cassette-recorder, and a warm wind blows. After a week of these African winds (which can last for a day or three weeks) most of the travellers and tourist have left, so the village is peaceful. On a June evening, we all sit down to eat; Ben, a trainee solicitor, with bright blonde hair, freckles and an Irish-looking face, sits opposite Vannila, a Jewish High School girl, with long thin brown hair slipping over her shoulders to reveal large freckled bosoms. She alluringly slips the dress back over her shoulders, in the manner of Scarlet O'Hara, as she mimicks the part of a struggling West-End actress. She is witty and feminine. Next to her, sits her buxom sister as if she is waiting to join the hunt, eating the meal with relish and savagery. The Aussi traveller passes the bowls of various dishes along the table and the sister tucks in to each one. The port-like village wine is poured, and we all expect a pleasant relaxed evening. In this romatic situation we are all intoxicated and are enjoying each other's company, when up the spiral stairs comes Marianna! zee Peep-show artist. In his "conservative" and reserved way, Ben thinks that she is crazy, and for all intents and purposes he is correct. I, in my naivety, offer her a glass of village wine, and a seat (she never sits down in company). She laughs, in her mad way and gulps back several glasses of the vino. Then she turns up the music, strips and does a Gogo dance. She loves attention like this. She pulls me up to dance. I pretend that everything is funny and supress any erotic urges. The English girls are shocked and embarrassed by Marianna's display, but Ben just laughs. I sit, to get away from her. Suddenly, she leaps half naked on to my shoulders, laughing and facing Ben. He can't believe his eyes, full with the intimate parts of her body, which wrestled with my neck and head. The English girls disperse and Marianna goes to bed after ex-

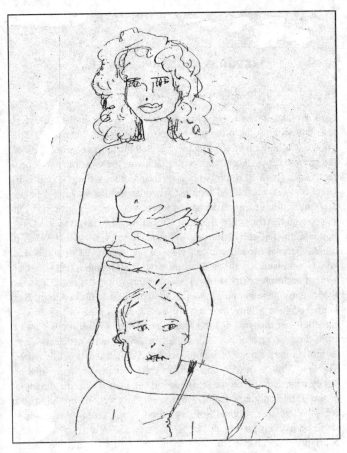

Marianna - peepshow girl.

hausting herself. I think of following her, but change my sensible mind.

"What a picture!" Ben laughs. Poor Marianna got the blunt edge of everyones criticism! Then we all retire to our bunks on the open roof, chat and watch the moon fade behind the hill, after that blood red sun had sunk swiftly into the sea, dropping below the horizon line.

Gavdhos and Gavdhopoula

Romance and Shopping in Crete

Next evening at about six o'clock we were all sitting on the hostel terrace overlooking the olive groves, the valley and "Pirate Bay". The village was high up on the hillside, and had the most beautiful view of the sea and capes. Not in the sense that it was the most typical or perfect view. There were probably a thousand other settings like this in Crete and elsewhere, and hundreds of other similar looking villages and much more pleasant in appearance. We were facing the Libyan sea (beyond, Africa) and the faint Cretan islands, Gavdhos and Gavhopoula, the tail-end of Europe. What made the view special? Was it the Archetypal Medditerranean view of our dreams? This place was "the Good Place" (as the Irish writer would call it) and it had a special kind of atmosphere (most travel book writers would not notice this, as they went village hopping). As if something saintly or wonderful had happened here a long time ago. Was it a holy or ancient site? The traveller had this feeling: the tourist, a feeling of well-being, away from the problems of home, but the true source remained a mystery; as more contrete hotel blocks blocked and dotted our beautiful view. The Lost Village of Mirthios was out there somewhere in the hills or valley near the cape on the left-hand-side and perhaps in the direction of the Hotel Panorama. But less serious matters were on our minds, as we sat there in a relaxed holiday mood, sipping red village wine, some of us with merely fleeting impressions. We were pleased that Marianna was absent from the scene and I that Cecile, the Dutch woman was present. Her face, I fancied straight out of a Dutch-interior in oils. It was a sight for sore eyes, and she was a pleasure to talk to. She would call some of our conversations at Nikos's bar: "Our Dream Talks"... Lovely English! The night closed in, and we all unwound, sitting outside, one of the joys of Crete.

Love was far from my mind, but in fact close at hand. We laughed and told stories and Vannila twisted strands of her long light brown hair into curls by her ears. She had a girlish creamy white colleen-like

STORY BOARD

Story-Board.		Script.		Titles	
panoramic view of plakias	georgios taverna exterior	pan-in hostel	the mill & hills river	the bridge	Waterfalls Rocks Roof-thrush.
1. Irish-voices & music. the river meanders down to plakias.	plakias bay & environs comingin. fishing-boats comingin. 3.	authors 4 monologue	Irish river 5 music	6	River at bar 7
8, Irish-Music—9.	10.	(Change= Cretan Music	Cretan Music	the fisherman giorgio sits at bar. 11. Cretan-faces. angelo puttingon recordsby	backview. ——13
interior taverna; cretans tourists 14. Cretan-Love Songs——15.	moma granny in kitchen ——15—	table outside door. mattresses: blow off roof past taverna windows granny chasing.——	view of bay through taverna door. ——16—	exterior taverna. cars-lorres old-fathertime passes. ——19—	women children ——18 ——20
The weeman in cretan dress sits opposite Scots. 21.Lively Cretan Music 22	cardplayers at the tables. Enter the Scots & Georgio Jokigi Scots. 23 Bar	enter the dutch women. bar—— 24.	Paintings Tavernas walls, Loftisong subtitle 25.	Exterior Tables candles Long subtitle germens. cretan 26.	fisherman at bar. enter germens. cretan conver 26.
Olive-trees & nets 27.Cretan-music station.——28.	men &woman donkey&bow walking olive-groves. 29.	the small mill nudes. & garden. 30.	sea&rocks nudes. Lefkoyia-hippeys sea-taverna. 31.	Dammoni beach scenes bathers sup 32.	Dammoni taverna crowds.. Amoudi Beach 33.
India—— West-Africa—North-Africa—Crete—Spain—Ireland—Scotland—					

face with a lovely smile and she was just seventeen. The wine had taken effect and I invited her for a friendly walk up towards Sellia. The previous night (she told me) how a middle-aged Cretan man had chased her around the sink room, and she had given him a kick! My head cleared as we walked under the moon and stars. I never really knew when to make the first move with a woman, when to hold her hand or embrace her. There is always that uncertain moment of truth or rejection. Now the attraction must have been mutural as quite unexpectedly, we were holding hands, though more than likely, Vannila had initiated things!

But in Stravros romance was easy, with no need to think about it. Sometimes, I would be surrounded by females competing for my attention. I think this was because I felt so at home here in the village, relaxed and laid-back, and there were more comparisons and connections, as I later found out. The Irish cottages painted in bright reds and greens on doors and windows nd lattices. In Kinsale the fish shop has a large Minoan-like fish painted on the shop front. There couldn't be any connection? Was I making the same mistake as Sir Arthur Evans-rebuilding the past in the image of my imagination? In Stavros I painted large sunflowers and Minoan fishes on the hostel wall, just for a few free nights board. Where was this imagination finding its inspiration?

Celtic music had come from Mesopotamia, via India, Africa, Crete, Greece, Spain, to Ireland and Scotland. I played some Irish jigs and reels to the Cretans and the old men tapped their hands. Sitting there in Stavros in the long evenings or walking with Vannila, such fancies passed through my mind. It became darker by the road-side as we passed the bend by the olive trees and grassy patches with the sound of the village stream gushing down. We embraced and kissed. She was twenty years younger than me, ripe and full of feeling with warm breasts on a slim figure. She was somewhat innocent, but educated to know her place in society via University and a bourgeois marriage. I didn't realise that she fancied me, but I knew she liked me for being funny, an Irish artist or some-such mix. The age gap didn't matter out here in Crete. Old men still pursued young women and vice versa. She was well spoken and intelligent and so it was easy for me to talk with her. She came from a broken home, so maybe I was a sort of father figure. I liked her wit and courage and femininity and it was easy to fall for her. If I was rich I would have married her and lived in Crete. Nothing would have been better and my head was full of impractical schemes, away from the social pressures of England. The local men thought the affair was great. Old man pulls young girl. We stopped and embraced under the Cretan moon and made love on some prickly grass in a desperate and disorderly fashion, thorns and brambles scratching her bottom and my kness, but it didn't matter. We strolled back to the Taverna, kissing affectionately, stargazing and now lovers. Our friends didn't guess what was going on until after it happened. Initially, I wanted Cecile, the first woman I met in Crete, but she was in love with someone else. As I waited, she said one evening at supper "You can, anytime you like." We were good friends but I had misunderstood her advice. I thought that she meant that I should make love to her. But she had only suggested that I was free to find another. So I was to be her best friend, and we had long conversations at the bar and at the end of the evening she would discretely disappear and meet her secret lover with his black hair and sometimes, black boots, shirt anf trousers.

I was now very happy to have a young attractive girlfriend. We returned to the hostel late and everyone was asleep; Vannila needed to keep our affair secret from her sister (otherwise her mother would find out), so we went to bed separately and later in the night she would, to my anticipatory delight and desire slip into my bunk bed.

The hot breeze blew into the room like a hot fan and we were both drenched from the heat. We were alone except for Marianna in the other adjoining room, of whom I had forgotten. Vannila was soft and warm, I caressed her hair and we made love in the dark; her breasts were over-large for her slim frame. To her they were an uncomfortable nuisance, but to me a feast.

Her friend later warned her of holiday romances, but I wanted her to be my mistress and girlfriend and I, over the top, contemplate marriage, despite the gap in experience. Only the advantage of wealth would have made this a possibility. Our rhythms and love songs wake Marianna next door, she screeches something in German and English and leaves distraught, complaining in a sad hopeless way. She is sensitive and looking for attention and love, just like me. My affair with Vannila was bound to be ephemeral and so, exciting. I would go for moonlight walks with Cecile, when Vannila was away walking down the Samari Gorge. Ceciles relationship was also impossible. She would never with her brain and education be a village housewife! There were always new women in the village, from all over the world, various and romaticaly inclined; a bachelors paradise, if one was satisfied with the hedonistic tourist girls, though there was always the possibility of meeting someone with a more serious intent. As I pondered, downstairs in the bar below, the usual drinking and talking session was going on. Vannila and I fell asleep for a couple for hours, then she returned to her bunk next to her sleeping sister. While we slept, Moma and Popa were rising with the dawn, as all the village would. At the back of the village, a wholly different kind of life was going on, involving hundreds of Cretans, whom the average tourist never came upon, unless he stayed long enough. The locals worked and lived apart from the tourist life, which flickered around the main street, two shops and bars. On Sundays one would hear early in the morning, the sound of singing and praying coming from the church and occasionally see the priest in the bar. Likewise, in the other villages in the mountains where tourism little affected the way of life. Back in England it would have been practically impossible for me to move in Vannila's social circle. Despite my pedigree, I could not be introduced because of my penury bohemian position, not to mention, the age range of her school friends! I was talented, educated, but in effect a disenfranchised bourgeois, plus being Irish and older than her. And so I lived on the edge all the time, like the young people who sought the cheap alternative life. Later, I would meet Vannila in London in her High School uniform and we were worlds apart, whereas in Crete, the social and economic pressures were off... I had not contemplated chasing teenage girls. On one occassion, a fifteen year old Dutch girl had approached me and I just laughed at her. Cecile was surprised when she found out about my affair and Marianna said something to the effect. "I didn't realise that you were a dirty old man, I thought you were just a joker!" (I had been wearing English National Health spectacles and looked a bit like Woody Allen). Now, I was just crazy about Vannila. In Stavros, the mobile shops were arriving one by one; the chair-van, the vegetable lorry, the clothes shop, all with loudspeakers blaring out Cretan music, which alway woke up the late sleeping travellers... The music resounded;a new day in Crete and so much to do! Morning; Wake up! Sunshine coming through the hostel door. Turn on the cold tap: Kalimera! I shave myself with soapy-lather, outside on the hostelbalcony, with clothes-lines, plants and Granny. The reflection in the mirror is the new me. The new day: which thing to do? and the best thing - the reflection of Plakias Bay, blue sea and the capes; and thoughts of a day down in the valley, hills or beaches. The big Dutchman from Amsterdam says "Good-morning" and I smile. The street below is busy if you could call talking, buying honey, having a late breakfast with Nikos, busy! I dress and go down to the Taverna to eat Moma's French Toast. Vannila is sitting outside with her sister, and about to head off for the beach. I say goodbye, and Nikos comes and joins me, holding a big cup of black coffe. He smiles and says wryly - "Did you sleep well, Mr. Picasso?" "Oh Yes" I reply with a laugh. I always enjoy talking with him. It is not always what we say, but the way we say it. We have an understanding, even though I can't speak Cretan; but we could be friends anywhere. I never felt like a tourist anyway, and even though I realised I was a foreigner, I felt naturally at home. People and vans pass by; the dog pees against the lamp-post; the Datsun van is parked outside opposite the Taverna, with some tables from where one can view the View. People come and go, start and finish conversations. By now, most of the hosteliers have gone to the beach, or to Plakias - shopping. I, like Nikos, take my time.

Cecile is sitting at the Hostel office-desk waiting for new arrivals. She must wait until mid-day; then she will go to the beach. I pack my sketch-book, paints and brushes and swimming-gear, bid her goodday and set off on foot for Damnoni. I walk down the road - what joys, the smell of herbs, everything is new.

Oh, when you first arrive in Crete, there's nothing like it, getting on the bus at Rete, the backpackers, the Cretan people, the hustle and bustle, and off to the South over the mountains. The Cretan music and the smell of fresh air, the sheer drops over the ravines, the sun and the blue sky, as you stop at Lefkoyia and pass Asomatos village. Arriving in Stavros, home at last, the white buildings, the bright colours, the first time I painted the cape and sea, the wonderful hues. You live more in three months than you could ever live in Northern Europe, and time is full. Not tourist Crete, not Zorbas Crete, not the Crete of enmigration or the E.E.C, but the Crete which is protected by the African winds, the Crete of first arrival; the first time you draw the Weeman in Nikos's, the taste of the Fetacheese, the music, the moon, the

Cigarette-packet drawing, done, with the Scots in mind..

evenings, the senses of a child. It will never be like this again, or so you think! What else can God show me? But there's more!

I walk down the winding road towards Damnoni, past the Shell petrolstation, which sticks out like a sore thumb in the olive groves, its neon sign looking ridiculous at night, like some kind of spaceship. Behind me is the deserted cottage on top of the spiralling-hill; alongside, the black olive nets are spread out under the trees in the shade, green strands of grass popping through the gaps, stone weights in rows of meandering lines. A man under a tree is eating lunch. I go for the water tap to the far right of the station and gulp the water to quench my thirst and ease the effects of last night's wine, a glass of water for each glass of village-wine. The rocky road to Plakias is to the right, the road to Lefkoyia, Amoudi and Damnoni Beach straight ahead of me. The road in the middle, to - Rooms for Rent and also Damnoni and the big Hotel. I take the road to Lefkoyia. It's hot but I prefer to walk, rather than hitch a lift. When I get to the turning to Damnoni, it's very hot and I drink water from a bottle. On the corner is a small bamboo hut, which is a makeshift shop (selling melons), with a bed, table and chair. The area here is sandy with bamboos growing by a stream. Down this dusty track I walk to Damnoni Taverna. I buy a lemonade and sit and watch. It's busy with people coming and going to the beach and taking showers straight in front of me near some trees. I scribble some sketches, and enjoy the mixed company, guitar-players, holiday-makers, tourists, backpackers. A kind of hippy man in his forties, tall, with a relatively small girl-friend is selling homemade trinkets and jewellery. They live down by the River near the abandoned monastry of Ayios Ioannis, with the other Bamboo-people. The girl is about nineteen, pretty and tiny.

Time for a swim! I walk along the beach and see Vannila and her sister sunbathing. Vannila waves and I walk over and say hello. They are both bare-breasted and run out into the blue waves, and swim much faster than me - the age-gap, I suppose. I swim along the shore towards some craggy rocks, and swim back again as fast as I can. I am itchy with the salt and sand and from last night's lovemaking. And remember Joyce's - the scrotum tightening sea. Vannila is burnt red and covers her breasts with a silk scarf; her sister looks like a stranded whale, but she is jolly, in a horse riding kind of way. Its very difficult now, to remember what we said, but it was definitely small talk. Anyway, I am preoccupied, voyeuristically watching the various bare females forms. The Greek families from the mainland do their best in ignore the nudists. They find them uncivilized, and keep to themselves, playing with their children on the sand.

Vannila invites me for a drink in the taverna and we hold hands. We sit and talk, until her sister arrives, and then become more formal. Her sister leaves for Plakias, and we relax again, talking about the Village, and whether one could live there permanently. Cecile comes up from the beach; her hair is short, bleached and fair. She smiles and says "I have a lift to the village, would you two like to come too?" We jump up and all get into the Stavros- Datsun. The driver has a thin moustache and looks a bit Mexican. One day in Stavros, it feels like Mexico or Cuba; another day, it behaves like Ireland or Spain. One of the young men has frizzy hair and looks Afro, as he sits at the bar (he was always friendly, and a quiet man). When you drive up the winding road; the cool blustering wind blows the hair and is refreshing. Moments pass and we are outside Nikos's. My hat has blown away. Cecile thinks it's really funny.

Cecile goes to her office and I for a shower. Too much sun! One evening Michaelangelo (so the retired English couple relate), with instant reflexes, grabbed a boy (as he fainted in the taverna) just before his head and body crashed to the floor. He had too much sun and too much wine! Now in the late afternoon, the hostel is quiet, with people sunbathing on the roof, sleeping in the cool inside, or reading, or drinking a lemonade, talking and looking at the paintings on the well. Through the taverna door, Cape-Stavros is visble. At sunset, the sun will slip swiftly down, and Cecile and I will share if from our bar stools. One night, Michaelangelo, the fisherman will say to me: 'Don't become a victim', a victim of love, he means. Once, a Cretan fell in love with a blond woman. She took him to her room , they made love, and then she told him to leave! He was so disgusted by her coldness, he picked up the wardrobe and threw it at her, as she lay on the bed!

For two years he drowned his sorrow in drink, and then one day, he came to his senses, and said to himself - I will never become a victim again! Oh Michaelangelo, if only I had listened to you! After my cold shower, I go up on the roof to paint. The acrylic gets hard with the heat; but I really get the colour spot-on. I can sense it, the bright colours of Crete, with a touch of black for the nets, and the black Cretan clothes. I put a touch of umber on the cape for the caves, which were the German gun-emplacements. Nikos comes up the spiralstaircase: checks the bunkrooms, looks at my painting, smiles and leaves. I sit and paint away... Sometimes Michaelangelo totally egnores me. Maybe he has drunk too much, but on other occasions, he can be very intimate. One evening, in late summer, getting towards Winter, he says to me "summer is gone, the bad times are coming - the good times are gone!" He is unpredictable, plays games and he is moody;and frustrated, because he is highly intelligent and creative; so village-life is too limiting for him. This particular evening, the taverna is quiet and mellow.

Michaelangelo sits opposite me drinking a beer. He lights a Greek cigarette, and says "How are you today?" "Okay" I reply, with a cowboy slur "Did you sleep well last night?" he asks, with an evil smile. "You're a bit of a Boy, Mr. Picasso!" I'm always a bit hesitant with him. He is a masculine and independent man. He might cut my throat, so I'm always careful how I approach him, but it's my problem. Once he gave me a vivid account of how an insulted man had nailed the perpetrators hand to a table with a skewer. "Where do you come from?" he inquires politely. "Oh, Ireland" I say, "I wonder, do you think Ireland and Crete are similar? I feel so at home here!"... He doesn't reply because he thinks such comparisons are pointless, but he wants to go to Scotland, because he sees how much the Scots can drink.

Michaelangelo knows all about Cretan history, the guns in the caves from the War, night time shootout games, the deserted villages, the Nazis killed all the inhabitants. The Turkish Mills down by the river, the bridges and hidden paths, the lost village of Mirthios, vendetta stories, village histories, El Greco!

The village in West-Crete, where the real Cretans come from, the men, tall and strong-willed and the women slender and dark-haired. But all this was new to me, I was green-eyed! Sometimes, I wished to be a writer and write it all down, but I was a painter! Michealagelo broke my train of thought, when he suddenly said, in an offhand manner "The Irish have been coming to Crete for a long time! They've built boats here for a long time past." What did he mean? "For the Venetians?" I asked. He didn't reply! His voice had been so gentle and kind. The Cretans are strong men, but they have kind hearts. I had always wondered, what my Mediterranean island was doing, with its culture and music, stuck up so far north. How had we got there and when? Michaelangelo was being secretive, Cretans could be so secretive! I had given up hope of any more information and was sipping the strong red village-wine, when he stood up to go to the taverna across the road, and as he was leaving, he said - to my total surprise! "I will take you to the Irish village tomorrow!"

He left and I sat there gazing at my glass of wine, and the Magritte like painting on the wall; with a skycloud steaming from a kettle spout, by a window, a real wooden window shutter from the hostel, stuck in relief on the oil-canvas. After the police from Sellia Station left, Nikos put on the Rolling Stones, and in a moment, the taverna was full, and full of life.

Vannila came for supper with her sister at about six-thirty. She sat next to me and stroked my hand under the table. She was affectionate and I fancied our future chances. Her hair was shiny, and her shoulders and face suntanned. We ordered a carafe of village wine, served with salad and lamb-stew. After eating, we sat outside in the warm air and breeze. Ben joined us and the dark-haired girl, who was doing the Australian Grand Tour. They all did it once in their lives; 'doing' London, England, Scotland, Scandinavia, Italy down the Boot; Yugoslavia, Greece, Crete, Africa, India, Hong-Kong, etc. I was only 'doing' the village and its environs. Vannila occasionally, caressed the hair at the back of my neck, mate-like, sitting close, as my girlfriend, so it was all out in the open now. I made jokes, but rather overdid the upperclass accent, being able to fit in anywhere, at least, as regards conversation and manners. She was hellishly attractive and I knew that Ben fancied her, despite his facial denials. He was closer to her in age and social opportunity than me, so all he had to do was wait until they returned to England, and she would be his. Still, for the moment, she was all mine. We took a short walk up the road again, and kissed under the stars, her soft skin under her dress moved me with lust. We returned to the tables outside Nikos's and joined our companions. The German with the Greek wife entered the taverna and said Hello; Over a number of years her family had been building them a house nearby, they now lived and worked in Germany, but whether they would ever enter it was anybodies guess. He was always really an outsider in the village, whereas, in Germany the woman could somehow be happy. Women could make a home anywhere, but men were territorial creatures. One day, Wolfgang, showed me their house. His wife and mother-in-law had a hosepipe and were watering the garden flowers and plants. We stood by the wall and some orange-trees. His wife was about thirty-two, slim with long armlength black hair. The two women laughed, and put the hose on us, showering us with cold water. Wolfgang bent down, picked up some stones and threw them at the women.

They ran into the house, laughing and yelling something in Cretan. It was a flirting game of affection and they smiled like they were in love. We went back into the taverna and sat at the bar. I amused myself, by studying the rows of banknotes and I thought how feminine and plucky Vannila was, and how she had a hard head for drink. I longed to be happy as I imagined Wolfgang to be, with a wife like her. Sometimes, a villager, on reachings! the age of thirty-five or forty would be married off to a pretty seventeen-year-old girl from another village. Mind you, Cretan girls grew up fast. To the Cretans, Vannila was, as were many of the tourists girls, a loose-woman.

One never saw very much of the marriagable young women. I think they were all under lock and key or working in banks in the big towns. Usually, the men sat in the tavernas in the evenings and the women stayed at home doing their chores. So we were in different worlds, but soon all could change, as a kind of global consumerism stretched out its tentacles to all secluded parts of the World. For the moment, I would find and draw the local-scenes and characters. It was a once in a lifetime!

After a days painting down by the River near Stavros and Sellia, I was drinking a few beers in one of the tavernas at Plakias. I didn't know anybody, so I was watching the people outside, at the rows of tables and chairs. There was the usual Zorba music here, the waiters serving outside, the tableclothes blowing, by the pebble-beach and furling with the eventing breeze from the sea by the trees. It was cool and getting dark.

I heard a familiar voice.

"Are you coming?", it was Michaelangelo.

"Oh, Yes," I replied, without thinking where.

I got into his van and off we drove past the umbrellered tables, along the darkened road to Lefkoyia, the headlights revealing the gold-leaf lit bamboo-trees. The tarmac road was new and soft; so I could hear the little stones crunching under the tyres. In we drove, into Lefkoyia past the Hippy pub where I had met various characters. One man was dressed like a Biblical prophet in a long white robe, with sandles, a beard and long brown hair. He carried a knapsack over his shoulders. I remember, I gave him some drachmas, and he bought some Greek coffee and bread, after which, he opened the knapsack, to show me a small piebald puppydog! He gave the dog some bread and told me, that green was my present colour of fortune, and that I must, to find my way, resist the influence of others. He seemed to be living on nothing, and said that he was writing The Cretan Black Book... He lived down by the river near the old monastry.As we talked (I couldn't believe my eyes!) a hippy rushed past on a homemade pony and trap. Where were they coming from, these people? We passed the

Partisan Pub, and I just glimpsed a white-haired man with gold teeth and a priest with taped glasses, smiling. As far as I could make out, instead of going left to Preveli-Beach and Cyclops Rock, we turned right and took a road south-west of the new monastery. But it was difficult to tell! Up we meandered for about half an hour; then the road levelled off. Through some hills we dashed by more olivetrees. After some time, without a word from Michaelangelo, a whitewashed village began to appear in the distance.

As we drove into the village, women and children in doorways, stared at us, as if they rarely saw even local strangers, nevermind tourists! There, at the crossroads, I could see a bar called Naxos, and next door a small shop with a sign O'Briens! On the other side of the street, was a long taverna, with a roughly painted sign over the front 'Murphys Bar'! Michaelangelo and I sat outside and ordered two beers and Metaxas brandy, from the red-faced barman. He spoke to my friend in Greek, but when he spoke to me, in English, he had a soft but discernable Irish brogue. I could hear fiddle-music coming from inside. I couldn't tell whether it was Cretan or not; it sounded like a jig. The Cretan girl singer was lilting away. The barman put a jam-jar with a lighted candle on our table and offered us some stew with chops floating in it. A dog barked in the middle of the street, the cottages had half-doors, and a priest (with a ginger beard) walked past. Father Murphy, I presumed. He walked with a shillelagh, gingerly along towards the chapel. I heard the words of an Irish song;
"Soft April showers and bright May flowers
Will bring the summer back again.
But will they bring back the hours
I spent with my brave Donal then?
'Tis but a chance, for he's gone to France
To wear a fleur de lis;
But I'll follow you, ma Donal dhu,
For still I'm true to you, Machree!

The alcohol was making me sleepy and Michaelangelo wasn't very talkative. He made a movement to go and I followed. I fell asleep on our return journey, and when I awoke, we were outside the oil-factory in Stavros.

I went and had a shower and freshened up. Vannila and her sister were in the Tap-Shop, the taverna just up the road. It had a beautiful view of the bay and was a good place to watch the sun go down. There were often small feuds between competing pubs; sometimes, the owners would not have spoken for years! It was interesting how the various families ran their businesses so differently. Some were very friendly but just wanted the Drachmas; one goodlooking Proprietress, in her fifties, would serve with a reserved contempt. The Granny would be really kind and friendly. The old widow in the corner-shop would act as if she wished you had never come in, but she was really quite kind. The longer you stayed in the same place, the better it could get. You could be liked or despised, or just plainly tolerated. In the end, you were just a foreigner; whether you spoke the language or not. Contrary to common sense, speaking Cretan probably made you more of an idiot, because the locals could then really take-the-piss out of you; especially, if you were naive. I had seen a Yorkshireman make a right fool of himself by trying to speak Cretan, Nikos just considered him a wally. Where as, the Scots just laughed and spoke mumbo-jumbo; made up Greek phrases from the Beano Comic like 'one spagettios!' The locals only respected you for what you were! though you could get another kind of Drachma-respect. The strangest sort of feeling, was when the locals treated you as invisible. But the sun, oh the sun, made up for these imperfections, and one just slid into life and I never stayed long enough for it to become humdrum. "Moma, what's it like down in Plakias?" "Oh", she replied "I've never been down there." She hadn't been to Rete for years. After a couple of months, I began to feel the same way. I thought of Rete as too big and busy; reminiscent of Oxford Street or Athens. I just settled in. I, too, began to avoid tourists; and took the mick out of them. A tourist came into Nikos's one afternoon and asked him "Is there any good hunting here-abouts?" Nikos replied - "Yes, Tourist-Hunting!"

I sat in the Tap-Shop with Vannila and her companions & joked about England and Ireland, in a sort of high-school, zenophobic manner, British is best and pickles and pork-pies, but it wasn't me to talk like this. We were all equal out here, but back there, I was always outside closed doors. In a way, they could not wait to get back to it, not to say that I didn't like them; on the contrary, I liked them, and England to a certain extent.

Vannila and I left discreetly and wandered into Nikos's. We smiled at him and ordered some wine. There was a tall, sandled man with thick glasses, a well-grown beard and a good crop of hair (he wore jeans and was in his early forties, English probably, with East-European parents). He was sitting alone reading and drinking. He had a terribly cynical look. He turned out to be a science teacher. When he heard us speak English, he came across to out table, saying, "do you mind if I join you?" "No" said Vannila, meekly. I held her hand. He began to attack her, with - I'm older than you, and other misanthropic and mis-ogynist intonations and implications. He had a chip on his shoulder and he had given up on women. In fact, I was not much younger than him! I came between them, but I was much too tolerent and lenient with him. I should have protected my loved-one and told him in no uncertain terms to get off!

Still, we were together, and she knew that I sincerely liked her. We were both glad when he got up and left. Crete could bring out the worst or best in people, their feelings, desires and emotions. The food, the sun, air, made you so relaxed; so if you couldn't make it here, there was no chance! This man was difficult to understand, but I tried to be charitable. As he said, "Out here people do what, at home, they would never risk". The thing was, I, as an artist, had been doing so all the time! All my life! Yet I still couldn't sell, even my acrylic landscapes, because they were too 'professional'; not even to live from day to day. The tourists wanted more graphic picture-postcard works for keepsakes; thus local amateur paintings were in demand. I mean, I liked this kind of art, but it was ironical and painful, that after years of hard work, I couldn't even make my bread and butter. I painted the hostel. I designed a Minoan restaurant in great detail - to be called the Olive-Grove. It later became the Rete - Why Not. Even the hippies were doing better! But it was encouraging to see the paint-ings in Nikos's taverna. Without him, the pub would have been noth-ing, and he kept it from going too commercial! My short time in the village, constrained by money, turned out to be a rewarding limita-tion. The tall sandled man was eventually turned out by Nikos for, supposedly, bad behaviour. He thought we were all against him, which was untrue! and I said to him that there was always an odd man out and one day it could be me. I never liked to see anybody victim-ised, but he was an oddball and sure enough, he might well have been persecuted. I always seemed to be defending people; you see, I could

70

grasp too many different points of view!

Vannila and I walked and talked and I thought her so feminine. I went to my bunk and left her in the taverna. I put two beds together and waited for her. She came later, when I was asleep. I heard her undressing in the dark; then she climbed in under the sheets. I felt her long soft hair over my face, breasts hanging, as she kissed my lips and face, sitting astride me in a tentative way. I was surprised at her movements, because she was so inexperienced. I wished to spend months with her so I could entwine our bodies and personalities, and teach her all I thought I knew about love. Yet, she was more worldly than me and I felt it when she said in a critical but kind way "Your a big softy, Brendan!" After a long time with her in the dark, she returned to her bed, leaving me exhausted and sleeping.

The next morning, after showers, breakfast and looking at the Cape, Vannila and I set off for the river, where we were to meet up with Ben for a Picnic. We carried, Feta-Cheese, Wine, fruit and bread. Down a secret meandering path we walked. She wore sandles and that flowery dress, which billowed with the breeze. The view was spectacular, the valley, the sea, the grotto, the mill. We met Ben by a small waterfall. I swam in the cool pool, but Vannila didn't join me. (It was beautiful place, but they both were thinking of England). She was too embarrassed to undress in front of Ben and me, together. In the dark, or by the sea with strangers, it wouldn't have mattered. She was tired from the heat and glad to relax in the cool of the riverside, and enjoy the beauty of natural things.

One morning, Vannila left and I was broken-hearted. We said goodbye outside Nikos's and she got on the bus, waving farewell. After about a week or so, I received a letter from her. It was extremely articulate, educated and sincere, but disappointing, a kindly brush- off! and not a loveletter! It was sensible in the voice of an older person, maybe her mother. I sat under an olive tree and wrote her an intense passionate letter, saying that I loved her and how we would meet again in London and carry on the affair. She agreed that it was much more than a 'holiday romance', but, we should, for the present, draw a veil over things, until we met again. The letter was thus so mature in tone, and sensible in outlook, that it made me feel, in comparison, overwrought and infatuated. Our time together had been so brief. She wrote, 'It all seems now, unreal. We are in different worlds'. My letters were, I knew, too desperate and too adoring. She had told her mother, but not her boyfriend. She said how she hoped that he, a plastic-surgeon, would reduce the girth of her bust, and I advised her against such drastic action!

Later in London, she would say to me "It should never have happened", she would have a new boyfriend her own age and she would be going up to Cambridge. At any rate, this is what she told me, as she sat there with her school books! Now, she was gone, and I sat at the bar, downcast. Nikos gave me an alcoholic drink and cunningly and kindly got me to do some graphic signs for the bar. I would so, get my mind off her, and later have a long interesting conversation with Cecile and go for moonlit walks, hand-in-hand, and really, Cecile, my best friend, was a million times better than anyone I had even met. (Oh Cecile, I missed out there! If you were free, there would be no-one else in my life!) Michaelangelo would say "Whats the matter, Mr Picasso? Why are you so "melancholic" - don't be a victim!" Cecile and I would walk along the road in the direction of Asomatos Village, both emotionally high, and console each other. We would discuss the Vendetta story, and the ins and outs of village life, its power structure and limitations, and the life of foreign settlers. Whether, she should stay or go back to University? We would have doubts about our rosy view of life here and our 'Dream-talks'. She was, apparently, cool and impartial in her judgements and I, emotional and intuitive in mine, or so it seemed, and she would suggest that visitors get carried away out here!

On the morning after Vannila left, I awoke feeling sad and looked at her empty bunk and wished I could make love to her again. Then sometimes, I would awake to see Cecile asleep, in her bed, several feet away. It was a beautiful sight. She slumberd, wrapped in a thin patterned sheet, all covered in soft coloured hands, somehow, like a Gaugain. "Good morning, Cecile!" - "Hello, Brendan!" We would look out at the ever increasing number of concrete buildings, and she would think of going home to Holland. One morning, she came to say goodbye, and kissed me on the cheek. I was painting and happy on the balcony, it was sunny, as I waved goodbye: Now, there was just me, on my own, my friend was gone! My only friend left was Nikos.

One bright evening, while drinking with the Scots, the wind was madly blowing. It made everyone moody, I looked out the taverna window, (Nikos was emitting a half-grin) to see Granny dash past, and to my amusement, this occurred several times. I looked outside, to see what was going on! All the bunk-mattresses, were being blown off the hostel-balcony and flying down the street, some disappearing like flying -carpets into the valley below. Granny was chasing them down the road (Poor Granny is since departed). I laughed my head off, at all these cartoon like images, I Loved it all. I would do, pretend magic tricks, not real ones but clowning joke magic. The villagers loved tricks and jokes, and had a good sense of humour, and I would take it to its limits. I wore National Health spectacles as a kind of protection and disguise.

It turned out, that people saw me as a lovable comic, girls as well! I would make cigarettes disappear through Wolfgang's ears and all the villagers at the bar would have hysterics. "Do it again, Brendan!" I would make coins come out of fruit, and burn Drachman banknotes and make them re-appear again, and suddenly, stare through the open taverna window, from the street at Nikos drinking with the Scots, wearing a Groucho Marx nose, glasses and moustache. The Scots would be full of fun and tricks themselves, and provide everyone with non-stop entertainment, with their lightning repartee. They got too much for Cecile, and their drinking was over the top, as was their breaking of wind. They were physical-training teachers, and we got on well. Lots of nice people came and went, but a few days before Cecil left, the ruin of my life arrived in an Ex Post Office van.

These were, a surly, drably-dressed man and his girlfriend who wormed their way into people's affections. They were looking for work, and work for foreigners was scarce in Crete, so the competition could be fierce. They wanted the vacant position as manager and they had the advantage of being two. I had painted some of the hostel and the owner wasn't satisfied with me. So when they got the job and I felt like, pushing them and their lorry, over the ravine. I tried to live with it and be nice to them, even though, I had been cheated; and the man would say to me, "You lost, You lost!" to rub it in. The position would have enable me to do some fine painting, and so the job meant a lot to me, whereas, they just needed subsistence money. It was a great shock, to find such people in what I believed, was an idealic place! and they didn't have any compensating traits. It was a social, open , community - for better or for worse - that was the thing I liked about the village people, they had their bad side but they didn't try to hide it, so, this couple were totally out of place. But the Scots knew what the villagers and other travellers did not see and what seemed obvious to me. My idealism had been cut, I had met my first enemies in Crete! So beware, traveller, its your fellow-traveller, who will steal from you, not your host! But, as it turned out nobody could pull-the-wool-over Nikos's eyes for very long! In two weeks, or so, he would tell them to "get lost". Anyway, dear Reader, to conclude this unpleasant anecdote, this couple did me, unknowingly, a wonderful turn, as bad changed into good, with mysterious repercussions!

As Cecile said later, "Nikos is usually 99% right about people's characters. Unfortunately for you, on that occasion, he was wrong!" So I decided, to go away from my beloved village for a while, to reflect. I left, without telling anyone but the hostel-manager (my big mistake! I was still denying to myself, the true nature of his character!). I left my suitcase, which contained my art materials and paintings, under my bunk.

That unhappy morning, I walked up around the back of the village, ashamedly and cowardly, avoiding the taverna in which the atmosphere, had, at least for me, gone hopelessly sour, and I made my way, rucksack on my back, sketchbook sticking out, to Lefkoyia, the partisan village, a totally different kettle of fish!, and from there to ponder my next move, my new direction. But as I walked out that day, I didn't know what new adventure was around the corner!

Stavros - the Film!

Scene (1)
Athens; panoramic view of the city, Acropolis, Greek Music.

Scene (2)
Six young Scottish teachers, lead by the eldest, BIG JIM; depart on boat from Piréas: The holiday begins.
BIG JIM says to ALEX in a Glaswegian accent - "I'm so hungry, I could eat my Granny's pissy mattress!"

Scene (3)
Time; Noon. Place: Mountain village - overlooking bay.
The bus arrives in the village of Stavros; locals; tourists with rucksacks, disembark, including the six Scots. A group of hiking German youths are drinking pints of lager outside the taverna. (There are several scattered tables and chairs). They listen to the Dubliner's singing - "Down the Rocky Road to Dublin". - which is coming from the bar inside. BIG JIM wears long red shorts and T/shirt (Slogan) BIG JIM goes inside first and gesticulates; 'I didn't come two thousand miles to listen to the F/Dubliners. The taverna is empty, except for an Irishman and a girl. BIG JIM smiles at the two, and turns-on his large cassette-recorder, from which comes Top of the Pops on the BBC and goes back outside to his companions.

Scenic View (4)
Pan along taverna and hostel.
Potted plants with Greek Granny watering, on second-floor balcony of the white glaring building (not unlike and Edward Hopper-US Artist). Top-Rooftop; 20 bunks with kipping hikers. Two girls look out at panoramic view of the bay, which has two peninsulas - left and right: green-sea, olive grove, valley below.
There are 3 doors leading into 3 rooms on the second floor; i.e. Granny's room (right) hostel office (middle) Scots-room (left). From here to the rooffloor, an iron stairway goes up in the right-corner.
Background, pop music.

Scene (5)

Past a row of 6 toilets, up 'Prompt-side" winding stone steps - march the 6 Scots, with BIG JIM at the head. The tall Dutch hostel manager (a young woman, wearing a black smock, in her twenties, with fair - short - hair, blue eyes; thin lips, smiling, greets them; "Hello". She refers the Scots to the roof - "Please use the roof beds" (Order). BIG JIM - pointing to the far room door: "This is the Scots room!" WOMAN; "Please go upstairs" Now, she politely requests them. The Scots ignore her, and unpack clothes; dozens of bottles of creams and suntan lotions. The recorder blars out 'Pop'.

Scene (6)

The Dutch woman sits at her desk in the office, writing and serious; having given up with the Scots. She had never met or heard of men like these! She looks up at the view of the bay; through a clothes line and over the balcony wall; on which hangs a red-patterned blanket.

Scene (7)

The Scots pass her view; BIG JIM and ALEX are carrying a crate of Whisky. Paul and John, another crate. They go down to the taverna to give their present to Nikos, the young Cretan inkeeper. Families take the afternoon rest on various balconies. Variations of this grouping occupy the variuous verandas and balconies, up and along the houses of the village, which 'step' up the hillside.

A chair-selling van arrives in the road below. The Cretan salesman unloads various sorts of chairs and turns up his music-loudspeaker. People gather round him and Cretan socializing ensues.

Scene (8)

The Irishman and the Girl look down from the rooftop-balcony.
THE IRISHMAN; "It's just like a Film!"
GIRL: 'Ja'

Scene (9)

BIG JIM embraces Moma - lifting her off the ground. Women and children come in off the street and join in the fun. The Scots go in the bar and shake hands with Nikos. They drink several pints of lager and retreat to the roof floor. Make jokes and go and kip in the Scots-room.

Scene (10)

On the Roof floor; The 3 non-drinking Scots are sunbathing with face-towels covering their groins. The Irishman is painting a view of the bay and sweating. The other tourists are bemused and embarrassed by the Scots strange behaviour. The Scots take over the whole atmosphere. Several hikers kip on the bunks, e.g. a Bearded beatnick with sandals reads a philosophy-book, a blond Dutch girl moves about restlessly on a bunk; she wears a mans, open shirt and flowery briefs. It's hot on the roof and a strong wind blows below the roof-wall. Several topless Swedish, German and French girls sunbathe on the concrete floor and sun-oil each other. Cretan music comes from the road below with intermittent traffic sounds.

Scene (11)

About 7 pm. Evening 'Session' begins.

BIG JIM, ALEX and PAUL, march down to the bar and order;

BIG JIM "3 Beeros, 2 Spagettios"

They sit down at one of the long taverna tables eating and make quiet cracks and comments. Moma is sitting at the desk and smiling - but looking tired and leans on her elbow.

Taverna description;

The bar faces the dining area and tables. It has a swing door on the side near the kitchen entrance, and a stereo-system at the other. A drawer under the bar contains objects. On the bar are notes of various currencies, pinned everywhere and bottles of ouzo, whisky, gin etc. and one giant bottle of Ouzo. On the top middle bar-shelve is pinned a sombrero, and at each corner hangs a stuffed-hawk. 'Backstage' is another dining-area, where mainly the tourists sit. (The centre of action is around the bar area). This area has 4 paintings on the walls. The first is in the style of Magrette, with a kettle and steaming cloud and a real lattice door; it is the missing door from upstairs, taken from the hostel office window. The second is in the style of Renault; by two classical watercolours.

The Cretans sit around in various groupings, e.g; THE WEE-MAN, a small man in his sixties, sits opposite a Canadian student, silent; the student reads. They are complementary! A group of Cretans, with moustaches, play cards in the manner of Cezannes 'Cardplayers'.

Nikos wears boots and Cretan traditional dress, as does the WEE-MAN. Popa and the priest are dozing, head in hands, at another table. Camera pans the bar, panning on; a map of Crete over one table; to the dominoes on another; to Nikos sitting at his doorside desk with

black, piercing eyes, and he winks! Cretan Lyra music sighs. The bar
has two large hand-pumps.

Scene (12)
Enter the hostel manager - CECILE.
BIG JIM: "Show us your beard-Glenda!" Cecile smiles cooly.
She goes and sits at the Bar with the Irishman.

Scene (13)
The Dutchwoman approaches the Scots (BIG JIM, ALEX, JOHN)

DUTCHWOMAN: "Could you please sign the book?"

BIG JIM: "Show us your beard, Glenda" then he adds in a serious
way "Later, Glenda!"

After dinner, the three drinking Scots stand around the bar and the
non-drinking Scots drink orange juice. They play cards and crack
jokes. One of these Scots ('Paul Newman') sits by an American girl
and chats her up. She is obviously available. His chat, in a strong
Glaswegian accent and in dramatic and intricate detail, consists of a
vivid description of a Celtic and Rangers footbal match; PAUL
NEWMAN: "Such subtlety - it was magic, magic, MAGIC!!!" He
bellows at her, referring to forward action in the last minutes of a
game. At the bar, the first bottle of Whisky is opened. The American
girl and an Irish (liberated) nurse, who fancies Alex, join the drinking
Scots fot the evening session. The conversation between the Scots,
Big Jim, Alex and the two women is rude and loud. They are well
matched!

Scene (14)
A group of middle-aged and older Cretans sit around one of the tables
near the taverna door playing cards. Moma sits in the background, in
the kitchen, almost asleep, after a long day. Outside, cars and lorries
occasionally stop; the drivers stop, pop in and go, Cretans pop in for
after-work drinks. Then home to the wife.

Scene (15). At the Bar
BIG JIM: "Coming up theTap-Shop?" to his mates - Alex and John.
ALEX: "Are you coming Glenda?"
DUTCH WOMAN: "No thanks boys!" Confident but blushing.
The two other women follow Big Jim and Alex.

Scene (16). The non drinking Scots at the Table (Paul, Joe, Martin)
PAUL: "I'm so hungry, I could eat a McDonalds!"
Laughter from the others.

The moon is brilliant outside over the mountainside, through the taverna window. Outside various Cretans, Greeks, Tourists sit at tables eating or drinking. A dog is tied to the lamp-post, barks, and pees against it in dog fashion. Cretan children follow their mothers home. One kid has a cricket humming inside two clapped hands. Moma goes home to do the ironing. Granny goes to bed, after watering a plant of unknown species!

Scene (17). JIM. ALEX, JOHN, return from the Tap-Shop. A bottle of whisky appears on the bar from a row of a dozen similar bottles situated on the bar-sheld. A French couple enter the taverna and sit at one of the tables near the bar by the door. The woman is darkhaired and attractive and looks a bit like Edith Piaf. The man is small and thin. He gets comically drunk and slurs his French-English, shouting in his funny angry way at the Scots and at Nikos.

ALEX at the bar
"Excuse me!"
He walks out the door and vomits behind a tree. He comes back inside and gulps a wee dram of whisky to quell the bitter taste of his spew. The drinking session continues until all are well gone. The French couple sit outside. The Scots and the two girls (out in the middle of the road) throw basins full of water over each other.

Scene (18)
Marianna, comes up the donkey path through the olives in the dark, flashing a torchlight. When she reaches the road outside the taverna, which, in the lamplight, looks like a stage-set. Alex grabs her and carries her over his shoulder along the street. She screams playfully. The liberated Irish nurse not realizing that all is in fun, has an argument with Alex, while Marianna laughs and giggles.

BIG JIM fills a basin full of icy water in the kitchen, goes up on the first balcony over the taverna; and pours it down over the Frenchman. Edith Piaf screams. She is wet. He is soaking. He runs upstairs to find the culprit, but without success. He rants and raves in his peculiar way. Nikos grins. He can't stand the wimp.

Scene (19)

BIG JIM AND Paul carry ALEX upstairs to his bunk, followed by the Irish nurse.

In the bedroom:

BIG JIM (diplomatically) "I'll be off"

ALEX (Drunk) "Stay! and see what a welting I'll give this one!"

Scene (20)

3 am. The 12th of July, Orangeman's Day.

The sound of shouting and singing comes from the village street.

From an upstairs shop window; A Cretan shop-keeper wakes up and shouts insults at the Scots. They march up and down beating a tin drum and singing - My Old Orange Flute.

NEXT DAY, Morning.

BIG JIM AND ALEX, with a Whisky hang over, go on a five mile run along the road which meanders through the olive fields.

BIG JIM to ALEX (As they jog) "I can't drink that village wine. It gives me an awful head!"

AFTERNOON. The football match between the Scots and the Cretans, takes place on a dusty pitch. The temperature is in the nineties, and the crack is Scottish.

The Journey
The walk to the Partisan Village and meeting Mona

That morning I left the village, and I walked away down the road past the Shell garage and past the tap. I was forlorn and sweating with the heat, now and then, gulping water from a plastic bottle. The bamboo trees moved with the breeze, and occasionally, cars and vans passed me by. The road was rocky and dusty, but I was relieved to be on my way. I paced fast, and carried my rucksack. I wore a torn-at-the-elbow, tartan shirt, and jeans; and the sound of Cretan love-songs, dark and oriental, panged at my heart-strings. But my solitary hike, mellowed my various disappointments, and I was coming to my senses again, no more emotional involvements for me! I passed, the turning for Damnoni-beach, where I picked a melon from a nearby field: they were rotting in the sun. I looked up at the Chapel of Timios Stavros, which was perched at the peak of the mountain and I thought, I would desist from walking up there for now. I turned in the direction of Lefkoyia village, where I knew there was a beer waiting. I came up a hill, by some small olive-trees, and along by some gushing water, coming from long, overground irrigation-pipes. After another stretch of road, which was tedious and much of a muchness, I perceived some white houses by some orange-trees, with vines coiling towards the roof of a veranda. A woman was doing her washing, and except for her, there was nobody else around. An old, broken-down, three wheeled van lay at the side of the road; it had obviously been there for many years. There were more houses, and I could see shops on each corner. All the shops were tavernas, but there was a place, which looked like the big meeting place, the kind of place which was used to travellers and tourists. I passed this, in my weary fashion between the two corners, and about a hundred metres away was another taverna with a man with gold teeth and glasses. He was standing and limping then he moved back into the shade of the bar. I stopped and said "Hello". At which he smiled and waited for me to enter, or sit outside, at one of his tables. The place seemed so quiet that I turned back, and walked

The Monastery

back down the street to the tourist bar. A priest with brown (national health) broken glasses, passed my path and he too smiled kindly. They obviously didn't care much about business here, you could take it or leave it and just do as the locals did.

I was completely worn out, and I couldn't see (I had no sun-glasses), so when I entered the taverna, with the eye-shock of sudden 'darkness', I barely saw a table to sit at and a pregnant (8 months) Cretan woman, who acted like she didn't want to serve anyone.

I dropped my rucksack, with my sketch-book sticking out, by the table and went over and ordered a beer "Ena Beera, Parakalo?" She seemed (not surprisingly so!) annoyed by my request, and about ten minutes later slammed a bottle of beer and a glass on my table, in an "unfriendly" way. Her husband, in his twenties, came in, argued with her, she had the upper hand. He shouted and left. She was about seventeen and attractive, with an insolent cheeky expression and dark hair. He looked like a good man who hated being in business and she hated being a housewife and pregnant and working, so they fought and later made up. She teased him and he allowed her to wind him up.

I lit a cigarette, puffed it and drank back the cool, intoxicating lager. It felt good and worth waiting for. I was, and looked, absolutely worn out and I didn't intend to move. This place was fine! I was so involved with myself, that I didn't notice anyone else in the taverna and didn't really care, after my recent bad experiences and love-jilt, but I soon became aware of a female figure, sitting at a corner table by the bar (had I noticed her earlier? I didn't know), and a deep female voice saying, to my surprise "Where are you going?" in Deutsch. When I replied "English?" she added "What are you doing here?" (I answered, but she couldn't hear me). She had short hair, with ear-rings dangling. She wore white shorts and walking-shoes. She was tall and slim and the ear-rings attracted me. She smiled, and instructed me with the hand, indicating "to come here and join her!" I didn't hesitate for a second! She was interesting, and I had walked into totally unexpected, company! I joined her and ordered another beer and she was kind and concerned, and like me, looking for adventure and new experiences. She was also an artist and so we had a lot in common, and like me she wasn't rich.

We made polite introductions, and I told her briefly my story, and what I was doing in Crete. She had been to Limni and Preveli, the year before, but she had never been to Stavros. She was camped down by the side of the river Megalopotamos and was alone. She had been there, for three of four days. I asked her, where her camp was. She said "Down by the Bamboo-huts at the river". "Oh, you mean with the Bamboo people!" I said, playing with her words; she smiled at my invention. I thought it strange that she was alone, and she told me of the rats there, and I felt sympathy for her. I wasn't that brave myself. I liked the company of people, but she said that her travelling alone was a kind of test for her, to see how independant she could be, and she admitted that she felt stronger for it. She had some feminist convictions, which were all the fashion at the time, but she was not dogmatic about her views. At this first encounter, we were formal with each other, though, indeed, friendly. After our initial introduction and talk, we walked together up the road towards Preveli and the river; and at the old monastry, we parted, as she wanted to be alone! We were still strangers. Later that evening I returned to the taverna in the hope of seeing her, and sure enough, about an hour after me she came in, in her shorts and long legs. She knew the owner and we sat talking

until it got dark. And still we talked and watched the goings on in the village.

The taverna filled up, mainly with 'alternative - life-seekers' (and the innkeeper played pop and old Sixties music), though there was the odd conventional couple on holiday. The atmosphere was good, and after a meal-for two, Greek omelette and chips, and too much wine, she said she had to go back to her river-living place, before it got too dark! I didn't fancy her chances in the dark, as she disappeared into the night. I had one last beer, and made my way to an olive-field, where I lay down alone in my sleeping-bag, under the fantastic stars. But I knew that the next evening, at about the same time, I would go to the taverna to see if she was there and I had the feeling, from the way she responded to me, that she would.

The next day I went on a long hike around the environs of Lefkoyia. I tried to walk to the palm-beach of Limni, but it was much too far for me that day, with the heat, and I never knew (I had no guide books) what curiosities awaited me there! I didn't even know its name, for I was using only my perceptual map, in my minds-eye. A conventional map would have hindered my natural sense of direction and adventure. My journey was one of exploration, as if no traveller had ever been there before. I enjoyed myself and my solitary rambles. I passed an old, deserted, ruined monastery, and wandered back to Lefkoyia village. I took pleasure in the landscape and the simplicity of things, the rough countryside, the olive-trees, nets and nature, and made the odd sketch of the clouds drifting over the lovely mountains. I came into Lefkoyia, along the street, which was pretty, with dark-scarfed women in doorways, looking out. Pastel coloured flowers grew in a garden, with a couple of tables, outside a minitaverna. 'Rooms to Let' signs were here and there and sometimes, a woman or boy, would try to get me interested. I loved the sight of vines and orange trees and the heat-reflecting, whitewashed walls. To the right of me, was the chapel, and to the left, the Partisan Pub, which was more or less empty. The priest was sitting inside with some women. I stopped and left my baggage outside near a table. The conversations were in Cretan, and so I could only guess at what was going on. The man with glasses and golden teeth, served me. I got a tea and a packet of cigarettes. He was kindly, and made a point of not being a capitalist, shouting sometimes at those other villagers he thought were profiteers. He showed me photos of his trips to the USSR and he was proud of his Bolshevism. He had been a partisan in the Second World War, and was now still commited to the cause! He served his time in the Resistance and now, ironically, he was serving the grandchildren of his former enemies! These kids were scruffy and hedonistic in their ways, wanting to dropout of the materialist rat-race, received cheques from home, make love and get high, maybe pick olives, and live in the cheapest places! So for the moment, the villagers tolerated them and some of these kids, I had seen being very rude to their peasant hosts! After the restrictions of Germany, I could see why they were so 'misdirected', but as an Englishman once said - Better a Hippy than a football hooligan or Shinhead!

I lazed in the sleepy afternoon while others worked or slept. In later years, I would work on the olive harvest, and get a very different impression of life in Lefkoyia. Now, I was content with just sitting and seeing the best, as travellers sometimes do! I looked over my sketches and started doing a drawing of the Lefkoyian priest, crossing the road. It was cartoon like and satirical in intent. Time was slow and full and unlimited. I was looking forward to going to the tourist pub in the evening, and was relishing meeting the German woman again. At about 5 pm I went down the main street to the tourist pub, I sat outside and got a beer. Inside, a long-haired youth was listening to some pop-songs. The innkeeper asked me in German what I required. This made me angry and I said, "I'm not German". Then, he said "What do you want?" in English. The village Lefkoyia had been invaded by hippies, who were camped all over the place and waiting for the olive harvest. On the wall of the taverna was a 19th Century painting of the classical kind, of a sailing-ship in a wicked, eerie storm. At this point in time, the village wasn't very commercialized. Michael, the young owner, had worked abroad and soon he wanted to return. He wasn't very interested in his present role and acted like he couldn't care less; so things were really cheap and often it was even difficult to pay him! I investigated the picture and its composition and it had a kind of antique charm about it, the kind of charm which is always psychological - not aesthetic! that which appeals to the unconscious, not to a taste for beauty! On the other taverna walls, were large posters of snow-covered moutains in the Alps!! I was sitting inside and feeling a bit lonely and waiting for company and conversation. Drinking alone is always boring and weird. Then I heard a familiar voice outside. It was female and friendly. She was speaking in Greek to Michael the owner. I must have been in the taverna about 15 minutes, when she arrived. She came in, smiling, and saw me. We both acted as if it were a surprise! I said "Hello!" and she ordered an ouzo and joined me. "Did you have a good day?" she said. "Oh, yes, I tried to walk to Limni, but it was too far!" I replied.

She didn't tell me what she had been up to. Then she said nicely, without revealing the meaning of her courteous suggestion "I thought that I would see you again" only hinting at any possible forethought of looking for me. I read between the lines, and we both knew that we had come in to find each other. Anyway, at the time, we probably didn't think about it,. only to the extent of being considerate of each other's feelings. It was her ear-rings, which attracted me to her and it was my sketchbook, which she saw first.

Her name was Mona and I couldn't help liking her, even though, I had not one week before been in love with another. Soon, it was evening and the taverna was busy and musical. We talked and got to know each other and I was proud to be with her. She was an Art-student in Bremen and she had just ended an affair. She had a Greek-Deutsch phrase book and was doing some drawing herself. It was great to have a female friend again. As for falling in love, I would try my best, this time, not to get heavily involved, but rather take life and love easy and slow. I would try to enjoy, as these German ladies did, the natural needs of the body and desires of friendship without getting bowled over, live the free-life of the naturist with the lovers and friends that you need, withour petty taboos!

In Germany, Mona had had enough of such Teutonic ways. She told me to take love easy and not to be jealous! I told Mona of my romance with Vannila, and how young she was. She advised me "Age doesn't matter! When I was 17, I lived with a Greek man of 48 for 2 years!" Her liberal attitude was refreshing in contrast with the puritan reservations of Vannila and her friends. Then I said, "What's going on? The village is packed?" There were lots of girls and boys dressed-up, and teenage girls in smart American styled clothes, maybe 100 people. This was a lot for a quiet place like Lefkoyia. Mona said, in reply "Oh, there's the village Feast tonight!" She was looking forward to it. I could see by the glint in her eyes. We sat inside with various other tourists and outside, at a long table, a party of French people were sitting and being demanding of Michael. The group-leader said "Take me to your kitchen! I want to see all your fishes!!" Michael was saying, apologetically, "I am sorry, I have only one kind of fish!" the French couldn't understand the situation and the sort of village and taverna they were in. They wanted waiter-service! They wanted French cuisine. They sat at the table in a group as I had seen other national parties do. At last, the pop stopped and on came Cretan and Greek music. The children were dancing in the street and it was getting dark. The atmosphere was real-Greek, not a put-on tourist show. Though it was a Greek occasion, foreigners were welcome to take part, which Mona did! She said "Excuse me Brendan, I must go and change". She slipped away and I wondered what she was up to. Michael stopped work and played his Lute.

All the village was in the street, talking, dancing and mixing. Mona returned wearing a dress, which was like a long T-shirt, with pink stripes, fitting snugly to her bottom. Immediately she was in a dress and made-up with blue eyebrows and a slight tint of pink lipstick. Michael and the other Greeks, were all over her, treating her with respect and making courteous flirtations. The local teenage girls usually wore jeans and sweaters (but tonight they were all dressed up) and they were dropping the old ways. Mona tied up her dress in a knot above the knees, and she jumped up to dance in the circle of Greek girls. I refused to join her, and so she was the only foreigner dancing. I felt that the Cretans wouldn't like her to take part but, even so, when she asked "Do you thing I should join the dance, I feel like it?" I said, "Go on - do it, don't be afraid!" Everyone laughed with pleasure as Mona danced around in the circle, arms to shoulders. The girls were made up and dressed to look much more mature and I thought she had great nerve. Everyone clapped and danced and the girls looked like women. Some would be married at 16. Mona came back to me and drank some wine and she looked feminine and attractive. The atmosphere was wonderfully friendly and it had that real Cretan flavour one gets at weddings and festivals, all the romantic side of Crete. The village was just the size for human-beings, though, the young people would have to go to the cities and other countries for work, so the population of many villages was depleating.

Mona and I sat the rest of the evening and watched, and occasionally, she would have a brief chat with some of the tourists and Greek people, she had met on her travels. Then we talked and talked and talked! Mona saw a couple in the taverna, a man and his mistress. She was intrigued by the affair, and told me how the pair had come to Greece to sort things out. We guessed at the outcome.

The walk to the River of Bamboo-huts

It was now dark, and we were both full of wine, and easy going, but we realized we must go back, somewhere, to sleep. We left the taverna and walked up the road towards the crossroads, which lead off to the River, Preveli and Limni. I Loved this little stretch of road leading out of Lefkoyia. I lit another cigarette, and asked her, as we walked into the night, "Shall I come and see your river place?" Mona answered "Of course!" I tried out my torch, but hers was better. It was a long, long way in the dark and even more so when intoxicated! But we continued to talk, as Lefkoyia disappeared behind us; but I couldn't imagine how we would find our way in the dark and wondered how Mona ever did so by herself; so lonely she must have been. At least, I would have been. The moon was huge, and drifted with the clouds, and we both admired it, and said many times how beautiful everything was!

It was a really long way to the river, along the road out of Lefkoyia, up to the crossroads and down around the bend towards the old monastery. At this bend, the sky, stars and moon were spectacular. The moon looked so big and round, we talked away and the walk wasn't too bad. Somewhere in the dark we came to a field with some trees and bushes, which the moonlight barely revealed. "Ah!" she said, "Here it is!" I asked, "What?" "The gate!" she replied, "We're here, at last!" and sure enough, there was a small wooden farm gate. She opened it and locked it behind us. Mona lit her torch, and we made our way slowly through the trees and bushes, and after a while, she showed me a gap in the trees and hedges and thornbushes, which completely covered the riverbank and blocked it from view. She said suddenly, "Take off your shoes!" Which I did. The river trickled along making a pleasant sound in the dark. Now and then. the moonlight would sparkle in its wash and pools. The water was cold to the feet, as we made our way along stepping stones and the bankside. Eventually, she stopped and said "Here we are!" Then I noticed a small enclosure by the river bank, with some camping gear. She crossed the narrow stream, to some rocks, where she had a cooking area and she lit a a candle on a rock. I dropped my bags and went over to her. I collected some brambles for her fire "What are you cooking?" I asked. "Spaghetti with tomatoes". Mona gave me some Camomile tea with Ouzo mixed in. I lit a Greek cigarette and relaxed. The taste of the tea was good and we enjoyed the river-sounds, and the jungle feeling it gave us. It was like being a child again, playing down by the river bank, Tarzan and Jane. After an hour talking, Mona said "Lets go and sleep!" "Okay" I answered. We waded across the stream to her bedroll and washed our teeth by a nearby brook. As we lay down, I wondered about the rats she had mentioned! There was just enough room on the bankside for two sleeping bags and the bank went at a slight slant, so I kept rolling into her. Mona said something to the effect "Can you please lie the other way!" At that precise moment, we were back to back. I thought she had meant, as there was little room, that we should sleep in such a way that my head was at her feet and visa-versa, in a 69 position. Then Mona said with surprise "What are you doing, lying down there at my feet?" "I'm doing what you asked" "No" she said "Not that way!" she giggled, "Let us... face my back!" I cuddled into her, but there was still not enough room. The she said "Get into my sleeping-bag, its double and bigger, it will be more comfortable!" I moved into her bag, and immediately felt her soft skin and as we touched, she reclined, quiet, passive and still in the darkness on the overgrown river bank. I kissed her and she lay still, which was surprising, with her independant outlook! I fondled her breasts and she didn't resist. We made love and she frightened me, the way she cried out, almost as if she was in great pain. I was worried that I was hurting her! She had many comings, moaning aloud a 'vaginal-song' of both hurt and pleasure, I stopped making love to her when she burst into tears and heartache. I said to her "Get it all out... Mona, let it all out, let it all out" After some time, she stopped crying and she felt better, she independant but she was also very sensitive. She told me later, I had said just the right thing to her, but at the time I just did it. We fell asleep, and next morning, I woke, to find her cooking breakfast over a fire by the river, and she was happy, as she said, smiling "Good morning". So this was her river hide-out! She looked as if she needed some good food, and good times! I shaved, and then she gave me boiled eggs and camomile tea, with a drop of ouzo in it. We ate, and enjoyed our surroundings. Life was simple and the sun shone through the trees. Later, we stripped off and swam in the river. Then Mona sat on a rock like a Nymph-Lolita, she said. I was staring down the river , which eventually led to Limni Beach, when I noticed some Bamboo huts in the trees by the far bank and a naked long-haired man and blond woman swimming. They were some of the Bamboo-People! I was surprised but Mona knew all about them! Could it be fun being a hippy?

The Old Monastery and the Hippies
at the Fountain

We dried, and packed our gear safely away, then we set off for the
village and shopping, up along the winding tarmac road. It was a
beautiful summer's morning, and I was amazed to find myself happy
again, after losing my teenage girlfriend. Is it so easy to change partners? Mona was all I wanted; and the language-barrier wasn't a great
problem for us. We just talked about everything, including her 'relationships'. On our way into Lefkoyia, we became very thirsty, so, she
said "Come, I will show you a spring!" The place was the old abandoned monastery of Megalopotamos. At the ruin, we sipped the cool
spring water under an arch, and she showed me the empty monastery
ruins. On our way out, we stopped at the spring to drink again and
when we were drinking some hippies approached us and spoke to
Mona. I was stunned by their hedonistic attitude, and mannerisms.
The two girls wore gypsy dresses, belly-buttons and pubes visible,
more-or-less nude with beautiful young breasts and long auburn, hen-
naed hair, tucked up with gypsy bandannas. They were beautiful, but
too silly for me, Mona was mature and much more interesting. The
hippy boy was wearing pirate trousers, and his scrotum was hanging
adrift from a rip in his crutch. I smiled with amusement and smiled at
Mona. The trio looked so theatrical and comical, but full of youth.
After a time you get used to nudity and freelove, and what sticks in
the mind are things like the gigantic moon suddenly appearing over
the mountain and chasing across the sky clouds, simultaneously with
the sun sinking, all in a few moments. Which amazed both of us, and
which was all the better because the experience was shared. Yes, in
other parts of the world, there were greater sights to be seen but for
now this was the best!

We were open to experience and willing. The locals seemed to take it
all for granted, including the hundreds of naked bodies; but when an
attractive woman came into the taverna, all eyes turned, so explicit-
ness is not everything! A glimpse of a Tee-shirt bulge or leg, can be
more eyecatching and with the landscape, ones senses were never
spared.

The atmosphere was so special to Crete! and on no other island in the Aegean had I felt it, not even in those early days in Santorini! It titilated and then absorbed one. We, the town and city dwellers, had lost touch with nature, and fantasy (as Mona pointed out to me) reigned! We couldn't relate to the Earth and we were soft. Think of the way the old explorers went up the Amazon, without innoculations and maps. And now we were destroying Nature.

We left the monastery and the young hedonists. It was getting hotter, and so it was hard work walking in the hazy sun. I told Mona how I had a Huguenot name, and she said, with the kind of surprise that only the discovery of coincidence can effect "Yes, I have as well!" I told her how many of these French people had been artisans and artists, and it turned out that her father was an interior-decorator. The tarmac was black and dusty and it bubbled with the heat, and I was getting thirsty again. We came to the village, and Mona took me to the mini-supermarket. The woman in the shop was friendly and good-natured, and we bought lots of cheese, fruits and some chocolate-bars. Here in the village, the food was simple, but so fresh that one could taste anew and one's sense of smell. came back again. The food was good and made the people healthy, but now they desired consumer goods and many of the things that we were fleeing from. Mona and I walked out of Lefkoyia towards the beach of Amoudi, down a narrow olive-tree surrounded road, and soon we got a lift in a jeep from a Greek couple. We thanked them, and found a spot by a boulder on the beach. These rocks were jagged and good to explore, and the rock-surface was warm, with small pools, and small deep creeks. The beach, the sand and sea and sky was inviting, as the waves washed gently in. We undressed and ran into the sea, swimming and diving like fish to water. The sea was emerald and clear, with fishes of all colours, and the seaweed moved to and fro. We came out after a while and lay on the sand by a freshwater stream. It was good to lie back, rest on the sand and relax without a stitch on and without a care in the world! I played about with the stream and made a dam. Mona laughed at my boyishness. We ate lunch, and the only sound was the sound of the sea. Then, she lay back and sunbathed, I rubbed suntan cream on her back and then hid in the shade by a boulder, out of the hot sun; it was too much for me! I later, took a walk along the rocks, by the small inlets; there was just the sea and me. It made me feel amorous, but Mona was usually the one to choose the time to make love;

94

it was just her way, and when she said 'No' she would be immovable. We had another swim, and decided to return to Lefkoyia. There seemed to be so much time. In Crete and Greece time is so long and full, a day is long as a month! She was silent and I was chattering away, which irritated her somewhat. We reached the village and we bought some more food. We decided to eat in the taverna. We sat outside and I sketched while she practiced her Greek. The pregnant landlady of the pub was friendlier and she gave the impression of preferring to serve, regular couples. By now we had become just that. We even got extra large helpings of chips. We stayed until an hour before dark and after an inebriating bottle of Demestos white wine, we left and were soon at the bridge over the Megalopotamos river, where we stopped and looked at the grafitti and the bamboo trees. The bridge was 'Venetian' and arched over the flowing waters, and later in the week I would show Mona a place of three bridges, which was undiscovered, and surpassed this river in beauty and atmosphere. Soon, Mona would have to decide whether to go her own way or whether to come with me and share my explorations of the newly, found out gorge and river!

Down the Road to Hedonist Beach
and Cyclops Rock

We got back to our river camp before dark and sat drinking ouzo-tea, eating and talking. She asked me "Tomorrow, I will go to the beach by the river of palmstrees, would you like to come?" Mona was, at this time, my guide and host, and I wasn't sure if she wanted to be alone again, so I didn't want to push myself onto her "Yes, I would love to! if you don't mind my company?" "No, please come. It's all right, really!" She added, "So, tonight we will go to sleep early and get up early!" In the morning, we had the usual breakfast, packed some clothes, and hid the rest of our gear. We walked along the road towards 'Palm Beach' and after some time a Cretan van picked us up. It belted and swerved, along the mountain road and I was a bit un-nerved, though Mona enjoyed the danger. Before long, we came to a gap in the hills, where there was a cove with the sea straight out be-fore us. On the left was a taverna on a slope and on the right the be-ginning of a cliff-top path. We thanked the two men in the van for the ride, and walked up the steps to the taverna. We sat and sipped a beer. The coast of capes, peninsulas and beaches went along for miles, and I wondered what was on the other side of the cliffe and hills to our right. After a short rest, we walked along the rocky beach, and up through the rocks to the cliff path. Some people came towards us and pased our way; so there was something of interest on the other side! We came to a narrower part of the path, where we had to jump, or carefull walk along a ledge. It was, at least a 70 metres drop to the sea, and one slip, and you were gone! I had no nerve for these kinds of heights - vertigo! Anyway, I made it, and after a short walk, we saw a beautiful beach below, in the distance, at the far end of which was a kind of stone hut.

We climbed down to the sands. The beach was wide, with a river end-ing its course by a little bridge and bamboo trees, in a small gorge at the back. The hut was a shop! and the beach was covered, though not crowded, with sunbathers of all shapes and nationalities. There were some caves in the far cliffs and not far out in the sea was a 10 metre high rock in the shape of a neck and head, the seawater just coming up over the shoulders. It had been carved out by the tide, and at the forehead of this bust, in the middle of the brow was a large eye! This was Cyclops Rock and here was Hedonist Beach!

We found a spot and lay down. Everybody on the beach was nude, so Mona insisted I join in. She had small breasts and a slim figure. I wondered if it were polite to gaze at the different female forms. I said "I could come now into the sand!" and she said "Do". We turned around to lie on our stomachs, and in front of us were a group of Athenian Bourgeoisie. These young people were tanned brown. The girls wore bikini bottoms which were high at the hip, G-strings in black, and buttocks protruding. They lay or stood, in a posing fashion, striking erotic stances. We pondered on this exhibition. Mona broke the silence "See how they pose, like Playboy models!" "Oh yes" I agreed, "As a writer said, even nudity is a kind of dress - so I suppose they are really in costume, you know the story of the Emperor's new clothes?" "Oh yes" murmured Mona in a reflective way. Yet, the dramatic urge was characteristic of Greece, everyone posed and made impressions; men, women and children. One day, at Plakias, a party of school-children came on the school bus, on a day trip to the sea. When they were about to leave, (I couldn't understand what they were saying, but I could see what was going on and guess the dialogue), one or two of the school kids from Rete were lost. Cecile and I watched the whole scene from the bus-stop cafe at Plakias. The head-teacher was screaming "Where are those boys?" One student replied "They're out on a rowing boat Sir". "Go and get them!" One of the older boys volunteered. The bus was about to leave. All the school children were arguing and shouting; the teachers were yelling at each other! It was all so dramatic, itcouldn't have been scripted better!

It's impossible to describe adequately without knowing Greek. It was living theatre! Everybody interacted perfectly. The big lad ran out along the front, screaming and gesticulating with his hands, along the pier, he got a rowing boat, rowed out and brought the two stray boys back. They ran along the front, the tourists and local Greeks all joining in and laughing. The coach was about to drive away and they jumped on, the other school kids waved out of the bus windows, all making individual comments, and everybody had a speech and a part to play. The headmaster gazed relieved, the locals and the tourists all applauded and we, the audience, cheered and clapped! So even in a small crisis everyone in Greece is allowed their say, down to the very pauses between each speech or line. On the big sailing boats across Aegean to Crete, when a discussion or argument starts, initially between maybe two people, others, friends or total strangers, may join in until maybe twenty five his people are weighing the ins and outs of a particular point or suggestion, and everybody in the discussion will stop when someone takes democratic turn to give his views, or opinion. It's wonderful to see. It's wonderful to be in Greece, where people actually talk to each other and everyone is given a say!

In the early evening, we made our way along the cliff path to the taverna, and we were in high spirits. Mona was difficult, moody and a bit selfish at first with me, (as she later said), but I stayed calm, until she loosened up and relaxed. She was now happy at being in her chosen spot and I was content to be with her. We had a meal in the taverna, got merry and laughed. Coming back over and along the cliff path was risky by torch-light, but I didn't care, except for that one dangerous gap with a sheer-drop, which one didn't worry about in the dark with the effects of the drink!

The next day, in the clear daylight, I looked and couldn't believe my eyes. It was so far down to the sea, and I climbed along that ledge! Never mind breaking your neck, it is bad news to even break an ankle out here, far away from a hospital! But we climbed along it every night. At a certain time each evening, we had the urge to 'go out' and the cliff top walk didn't stop us. On our return, we lay on the sand and I tried to make love to Mona, but she said definitely "No!". "It's so lovely out here, what a waste!" I pleaded, but still she wouldn't. She would make too much noise on the crowded beach? The sea splashed as we fell asleep and all was silent.

After our trip to Hedonist Beach, we were going to go our different ways, but Mona hadn't yet decided what to do and I couldn't read her mind. Still, I liked her and wished we didn't have to part. In a way, I really wanted a permanent partner, and hoped this relationship would continue, and she said "If we lived in the same country, there would be no problem at all!" She reciprocated, when I said "Mona I have to stop myself falling in love with you!" "And I with you, Brendan!" As we spoke we stopped in our tracks, on the edge of the cliff top path, then continued and later stopped again. So every night, we took the risk and walked to and from the taverna and life was good. I'm sure that even now, she looks back with a smile at our good times.

I told Mona of my island people and their troubled history, and how Crete reminded me of the homeland I had to leave, my memories of its music and people and its easy-going ways. She sympathised. As we strolled slowly in the dark, she said to me "At first I thought that you didn't know what you were doing, that you were soft, but it's not true, is it Brendan?" "You have shown me things I would never have found alone! Early on you were so patient with me. It was so good for me!" I knew then. Mona had already decided what to do! The moon was full again, and I always felt good and lucky when it was so, the sky clear, and the way clear ahead.

99

The Walk to the Monastery and Tranquility

We packed again and made our last walk up the cliff path. I didn't look back. It was a long highway along the cliffs, past the beach, to the road to Preveli, but eventually we reached this road and walked out into the open countryside, leaving behind Hedonist Beach and Kourtaliotiko Gorge with its wartime stories, where the monks had planted the palm trees. The weather was mild, as we strolled, with the strong smell of herbs. But very gradually, there was a strange odour, like burning or charcoal, and it completely dispelled those herbal scents! I noticed how the grass was slowly getting blacker and the trees almost imperceptually dark and torn. Very soon, everything around us was black and burnt. All the plants and trees, dead! You could see smouldering cinder woods and smoking embers, the fields began to look like the aftermath of a war. What had happened to Preveli Monastery? We didn't know yet. We walked on and around a corner, where we saw a whole valley burnt, with the odd tree sticking out of the coal-black landscape. We walked along in silence and were amazed at the sight of what had happened. A forest fire must have ravaged around an area of many miles. Whereupon, we came in view of the Monastery of Preveli. The valley around it was black and burnt! It stood on the top of a hill, with three trees still alive and green! It looked as if the fire had stopped or had been stopped, right at the doors of the monastery! Maybe it was the army, maybe it was the wind?

We walked up to hillside monastery. The sun was fair, and as we entered the place, a beautiful atmosphere of tranquility prevaded the whole area. We sat and contemplated the scene. The only other visitors, were some pilgrims. They were talking to the only available monk and he was obviously saying "Look what the tourist have done!" He was angry, as he pointed to the black valley beyond the monastry walls. This upset me, as I really cared about Crete. I regretted that Mona was unsuitably dressed, in shorts, for this holy place and I felt scruffy. We entered the small chapel, the priest was reciting prayers to a Greek couple, candles were lit. and the devotees made us feel completely invisible. I hadn't the courage to say a prayer, and I toyed with the idea, thinking it might have showed my sincere respect! In a corner was a shrine, with small plaster arms, legs, noses and other parts of the body. These were prayertokens, relating to various illnesses, requests for divine intervention! So Dali wasn't that original after all! The Greeks and the monks must have thought us, not only foreigners, but also complete Hedonists and Pagans - if not infidels! The monastery was peaceful and serene, out of a different time and dimension, away from all the noise and consumer materialism of the cities, the world, which was burning the rain forests and making holes in the sky. The world of wealth and poverty. So to the monk, we were like the Plague, itself. To the Greeks we were merely, troublesome tourists, a necessary evil. You see, the tourist had started the fire by leaving a lighted campfire. The fire had spread along the valley! The army had managed to extinguish it before it destroyed everything, and just at the gates of Preveli, the wind had changed! We left Preveli Monastery and returned up over some green hills and upland fields with stone walls.

Mona didn't speak, and acted, to my aggravation, as if she wanted to go alone. She would get into these moods and walk, as if I wasn't there, or simply make a point of going in a different direction. This time I had had enough of her moods, so I walked away from her, and eventually lost her somewhere behind me. I was content to be alone and enjoyed the lovely countryside. In the distance, I noticed a village hidden in the mountains; I didn't know that there was a village up here! I thought to myself. About the fire, I considered that the Cretans had no sense of danger or fear. They lived each day as it came, every day was a bonus!

I walked into the village and the women and children came out and stared at me. They hadn't seen a foreigner for a long time! It was an attractive mountainside village, all white, with blue and green doors. I didn't know its name or location, and I liked it. If I stayed up here, I would really be away from everything, but I didn't think that I could stand the isolation for long, at least alone. It was amazing how each village was so different from the others. This one was like an outpost, whereas, Spili, in a rain-storm was in another world with a completely different atmosphere. The people in each village were also totally

The tourist fire around Preveli.

different in character and circumstances and their accents were different.

Just because the villages were within walking distance. I expected them to be the same. There was always some more breath-taking sight to be seen or a new unknown village to be found, the rest of the world seemed to be taking on a global style.

I passed out of this village and rambled and meandered, until I came quite accidentally to Lefkoyia; I suddenly found myself coming down a side road and back street, at the side of the Partisan Taverna! I was glad to be there and the innkeeper (with the gold mouthful) was welcoming and smiling. I asked for cigarettes and Greek tea (with sign language and I guessed the rest). "Where have you been?" he inquired. "To Preveli Monastery!" "Ah, Preveli" he murmured. I showed him my drawing of the fire. He looked and said "Ohi, ohi, fire!" The priest looked as well and smiled, cleaning his old broken glasses. I was glad to be back in Lefkoyia, but I wondered where Mona had gone to! I went to the Tourist Pub, had something to eat and drank the village wine. I enjoyed some Teutonic company and watched the Greeks and the tourists and the hippies. By nine pm she still hadn't turned up! and I felt lonely and wandered back to her camp by the river. My torch was weak and dim, but with the help of the moon, I mananged to find the turning off to the river. I found the old medieval bridge, and eventually, with a sharp memory, the gate at the field. I struggled, drunk, through the bushes and trees, wondering where the gap in the big hedge was and where I could step along by the bank and find Mona's camp. I lit my fading torch and moved by intuition, feeling my way. I felt close to the spot, in the pitch dark. I stopped still for a moment, and then, I heard to my delight! A whistle! It was Mona, and I could see her torch beam in the trees. I followed it, got through the gap and there she was, candle alight, on a rock. When I got to her I kissed her on the cheek, and she was glad, excited, a bit perturbed and frightened but very happy to see me. She welcomed me. She was drinking Ouzo to calm her nerves! She gave me some and said, with distress "Oh Brendan, am I glad to see you!" "What happened to you?" I asked, "Where did you get to today?" I waited all night in the taverna, for you Mona!"

She told me her story... When she left me, she was moody because she was upset by the devastation the fire had wreaked and that blackness, after so much beauty. She was hitching a lift to Lefkoyia, when two men had picked her up in a van and had asked her to satisfy their desires. When she refused they got stroppy and drove her past Asomatos Village, well into some Gorge where she was lost. She had to walk all the way back, and had reached the river by another way, not anywhere near Lefkoyia village. In a way I felt happy, because she had become a bit helpless, bringing out my manly and paternal feelings. (That old caveman stuff!) My instinct was to be kind and protective. We were both loners and sometimes needed someone to lean on. It's natural and human to need a mate and a home! But on the morrow, Wednesday, we were supposed to go our different ways, as we had so discussed earlier, and say farewell to the village of Lefkoyia. She would go to the Pelopponese on the mainland, and I back to Stavros to paint!

I felt sad, but pretended not to care about where she went, not showing my tender feelings, but instead a brave, soldiers face. I was packing and prepared to walk up the road and bid her farewell, my head downcast, accepting my fate! Suddenly, she said out of the middle of nowhere! (Mona could leave important issues to the last minute!, drawing it out to the last second), "I have decided to come with you to the River of Waterfalls!" At her almost casual statement, I smiled and lit a cigarette and said "Good" also in a casual manner but inside I was jumping for joy and looking forward to the time ahead. I knew I had won. Through patience comes all! Not in the sense, that I was dominating the situation but in that, we were off in the right direction.

We walked to Lefkoyia where we waited outside the Tourist Pub for the bus to Plakias. I sampled a Greek coffee and nearly swallowed the grains. The bus came hurling into the village. There was a sense of great excitement as people got off and on, the event of the day! Within minutes, we arrived at Plakias, accompanied by many more tourists and backpackers. The sea was calm and the beach pebbly. We made our way along the seafront and enjoyed the change. The hotel with the swimming pool was somewhat quiet. On the corner, as we entered Plakias, was a hose pipe shower under a tree and a blonde woman in her early twenties was washing the salty water out of her hair, she wore a glossy laytex swimsuit, which shimmered in the sun. The cool water flowed down her, along her freckled arms, down to her toes. She had long thin lips. Greek music filled the air; the bouzouki sounds were full of expectation, as we found a suitable cafe. We sat outside eating yoghurt and smiled at each other. We were content to sit and look for a white. Mona looked happy but I couldn't always tell what was really on her mind.

Down the rocky road to Plakias.

Down the rocky road to Plakias

Many times would I walk down that rocky road to Plakias along that avenue of trees. It was one of my favourite roads to ramble down, past the rooms for rent sign, past the grape-vines and that little house with pink flowers growing in pots on the veranda. I would have given anything then, to have been able to live there, with some paints and brushes and a beautiful woman, the sort who would come with me to Crete and give up everything up north, but I never had the money, when I had the feeling to do it! The trees were tall and reminded me of a Pisarro boulevard. They began after the water-tap and there I did a perspective drawing. The road was dusty, the beach rocky, with heaps of rubbish the tourists had left, and they left everything, shoes, clothes, pipes and money. An old lady in one of the cafes had become, in relative terms, a millionaire! Then, there were the two bakeries, the supermarket, the disco, the rocky-jetty, the fish restaurant, the fishing boats, tourist washing, on lines outside rented apartments, overlooking the numerous taverna tables along the seafront. Then we rambled along the strand by the sea, along the sand all the way to the rocks by the cape, often lying naked in the sun. We swam in the foamy sea. The wind blew up the sand by the big searocks, by the road to the other beach, past the fish restaurant. Then we looked up at the villages in the mountains. The seawater lapped along the small jetty and I caught squid with bread on a line. I thought of the path leading to Stavros, the path leading to the river of waterfalls and the mills and olive groves. The way to the valley of gorges and the flowing mountain streams.

The athenian in this cafe was sharp and friendly, he had spent some time abroad. Mona was keen to go to the river of waterfalls and make camp. I showed her the secret path past the power-station and then the path along the river to the mill of grape vines, but I could sense that she wanted to be alone again, even though I had shown her the way to her dream river. So, at a point beyond the first mill, we parted, and that night I slept alone, after a few beers in a bar. I pretended to her and myself that I didn't mind, but really I wanted to be with her. I

Plakias Fish-Restaurant.
Choppy windy seas at Plakias.

Centerfold of Plaki

could have, at that time left her, and wandered off on my own but I
didn't want to leave the river and I thought, 'let's see what happens!'

She had some reasons of her own for wanting to explore the river
route. She made her way up the rocky stream, which came down
through the trees and boulders. It was good - she thought, to be on her
own again, though a few days was enough time to be alone, here by
the river, especially at night and being a woman alone! It was also
dangerous to be alone in isolated places, you could break an ankle or
become sick and how would you find help? She found that the rocks
got bigger as she got further up the meandering river stream, and the
pools became larger and more beautiful, with birds and crabs, and exciting trees and bushes, in all kinds of open and hidden formations.
On reaching one of these pools, she stopped and looked more closely
around. To her instant pleasure there was a cave in a rock formation,
hidden by some trees. Mona went into the small cavern and dropped
her rucksack. She sat down outside in the shade and ate some fruit
and feta cheese, followed by some Greek yoghurt. It was lovely and
cool down by the river, though it could be very hot, where the river
widened and from where you could look up and see the valley. Mona

…y in Panorama.

finished her meal, and undressed. She tiptoed back into the cave and hung up her clothes on a home made clothes line. She unpacked her small rucksack and put her swimming costume, suntan cream and anti-mosquito cream carefully inside. Then she put on leather sandles, pulled the bag over her shoulders and continued up the river bareskinned and slightly burnt on her arms, her breasts and bottom, still slightly bikini-shaped pale white. After a little while, she came to the first waterfall. It made a gushing, thundering noise which, except for the occasional birdsong, was the only sound to break the rivers musical flowing, which always relaxed her, especially at night-time. After a cold shower in the waterfall she lay on a rock, sunbathing for the rest of the day. It was good to be alone again, with no obligations and to be a free woman-independent!-making her own decisions. Mona, when she became bored with resting would read another essay by Anais Nin and weig it up and considered it thoroughly; (and sometimes later, discuss a particular point with Brendan.) As twilight closed in, she made a fire and cooked some spaghetti. As usual she lit a few candles after cutting out makeshift lampshades from some green water bottles, and hung them from some branches. After dinner she sipped Ouzo and Camomile tea, and listened to the night and the occasional fluttering bat. She was tired and so after brushing her teeth by a pool she put on her long shirt and got inside her bag. The river sound soon made her feel sleepy. She reached over and blew out a remaining lighted candle, which dripped on to the grey rock surface. She fell asleep, anticipating her next day by the river, being alone was good and next morning she could settle into her new surroundings in her own way... She rose, guessing the time, as she had dispensed with a watch to experience the slow time of Greece. Still, it was easy to oversleep here by the serene riverside. Immediately she got up she went under the freezing but refreshing waterfall, and then had a swim in its pool. It was like being a wood nymph and so sensuous. It was refreshing and cold as ice. Then after a few minutes of drying in the moderate sun and sitting on a warm rock surface her goose-pimpled flesh would mellow into a softer skin sensuality. Mona ate breakfast and drank herbal tea, then packed a bottle of spring water, sunbathing accessories, it was more convenient to be naked (except for sandals) she surmised-as it saved her the trouble of going around the deep pools in the river. There was a kind of logic to everything she did. That was her trouble! She often thought that she'd like to be more spontaneous, and so she sought adventure in Greece. It revitalised and rejuvinated her, so she could cope with the competition back home, and each year it got worse. The rainforests were being burnt, the seas polluted the ozone-layer was dissappearing, not to mention the greenhouse effect! Would Crete be next?

Mona, climbed and walked up the river. It was jungle-like, the trees making all kinds of exotic shapes. Some conjured up the Amazon and naked Indians or Australian Aborigines in their Dream-Time with painted bodies and spears. She imagined Greek Centaurs and nymphs dallying by the pools making animal love with their strange bodies. She thought of such loveplay and formed pictures and feelings of what it would be like to be half animal, horse, bull, cow; and how her body would savour the delights of such a state. But she often thought that the mental, and spiritual were superior to the physical; and her mother thought that he was weird for her age - "When I was your age, I was doing it three times a day! What's the matter with you, Mona? - You're a funny girl! then Mona visualised some classical paintings of Greek Gods in those medieval landscape settings. Cupids and rounded godesses with fleshy bottoms and breasts, inhabiting strange deserted ruins in sunsets; groups of lovers in the act of love. It was all suggestive. The real Greek painting were highly erotic.

Mona was tired from climbing and stopped as she came around a bend by a cliff. There was a beautiful pool with a cascading waterfall. She dropped her bag on a stretch of sand and swam across to the spring water. It was icy against her back and then it fell right over her head. Her nipples chilled on her small pointed breasts and after a few minutes, she dived away from the waterfall into the pool towards a small 'beach' where she lay back. She turned over dozing, the sand brushed against her breasts and fluff of hair, as she dipped her hands and arms into the shiny pebbles. The sun skimmed her back, and with the river atmosphere and its relaxing ripple sound, she day-dreamed of open-clams on rocks by warm pools and tingling sensations. There was only the river and her! With a slight shiver she stood, took a deep breath, bent and splashed some water on her face, feeling that her cheeks were flushed and her mouth and tongue were dry. Dreamily she tiptoed to some trees, keeping her balance on the rocks between the brier covered bank, by holding onto the strong barks and thick tree trunks. She lay down by a tree in the shade and stretched back, looking up into its branches; several times she tremoured at the thighs as she sighed with love for the river! After a short nap she slipped into the big pool and floated. It was only the river which made her feel like this!

After some further exploration of the river, Mona went back to her cave and dressed. In the corner, was a sleeping mat and a new knife. Who did they belong to? she pondered. She did some washing and hung it up outside to dry and then decided to go and do an acrylic water-colour. There was an ideal spot with pastel colours and a very old, large olive-tree (shaped like a human body, the lower half like a masculine Satyre) with mountains and a Prussian-Blue sky in the background. She wanted so much to be a competent artist, but the trend was towards a kind of Philistine graphic commercialism. Once the fine arts had been cut out completely, where would advertising get its ideas from? Then she thought of the Cretan villagers and wondered if the Minoans and Cretans were related at all? She forgot about the city and its busy life! After a few hours sitting painting, she felt thirsty and in need of conversation, where upon, she packed her brushes and sketch book and walked towards Plakias harbour. She passed some singular houses with gardens. After her long walk down from the river she came out by one of the seaside cafes. She saw Brendan sitting at a table looking out to sea. "Brendan!" she hailed. He looked around and smiled at her, glad to see her again.

"What have you been up to?"

"Oh, many things," she replied, keeping her secrets. I tired to guess at what they were! We were together again and it was evening. We sat in the Athenian Cafe enthralled in conversation and this seemed very strange to one tourist who stared at us and thought we were in love or something? Then I said to Mona," I was having a Greek coffee today and looking at my sketches, in the fish restaurant on the corner, outside at a table. It was quiet, with several couples eating, talking and generally looking at other folk." "You know, Mona,... when people are in other countries, they will do things they would never do at home!" "Those on short holidays are always slightly detached, as everything is brief-a passing image. They have no time to consider anything in depth." "On the other hand, they will have relationships and fulfil passions, they would not dare to at home, and of course, they never really see the country they're in. And they will do things with strangers, they never would do with their friends!"... Then I was looking at the fishing boats and feeling a bit lonely. When suddenly! MONA!! The fish restaurant waiter rushed passed me, stripping off his clothes, as he dashed and he dived into the sea. I thought that it was like a Martini television advertisement! with the freshest-fish-in-town! when he returned with some fish in hand! Mona chuckled with laughter and I stroked her hair, as I added "You see some funny things around here!"

In an hour or so we were merry and I was listening to Mona intentively and looking into her blue eyes.

Through the olive-groves to the Mill and River

A festival of Greek dancing was going on outside in the road by the tables and the atmosphere had the kind of flavour the tourists love, the Greece of the holiday advertisements; Welcoming Greek men and women sitting outside in the sun, village weddings, wine and white villages in mountains, golden beaches and green sea. Zorbas dance playing... and the thing was it was all true! Greece was the friendliest place in the world! Mona, unexpectedly admitted to me "Last year, I travelled with a Indian man, but he was too good and kind, so it was no good for me!" "Its much better with you!" I smiled at the compliment. I said "You told me that you lived with a Greek man, near Hania, Please tell me more!" Mona told her story. I had my arm around her shoulder.

"I was seventeen and he was forty eight. We were really in love!"
"How did you meet?"
"I was on holiday with a girlfriend, we were in a village near Hania, I saw him looking at me from a window, it was love at first sight! But he wanted me to run his taverna like a Greek woman and it didn't work out! I was too young to have children. When he asked me to have a baby, I knew it was time to leave the village; and he got jealous of other men, we would have terrible fights and then make up and make passionate love... in a most violent way!"
"Have you ever gone back to the village?"
"Oh, no I dare not. He would kill me!, We were together for two years and really in love!"
"Such an age gap", I interrupted.
"Oh, yes"
The wine was taking effect and we both felt it. The men who ran the small Taverna were cool but friendly, and they liked regular customers.

"Lets go, its a long way back along the river in the dark!" I said; and we set off down the path (with snakes) along by the power station, after which it got pitch-dark. Mona, lit her torch and I was full of "Dutch-courage". The moon was full and bright, but it was cloudy

that night (it would rain), so its lunar light was lost for most of the time. We crossed over a small bridge and turned right, to the path along by the river, to the first mill. The stream flowed, as we carefully climbed large flat boulders by the bend of the river, just before the bridge to the mill. After a few trips, you would get to know all the sigh posts, the natural ones, such as particular stones, bends and trees and the depth of the water. It all stuck in the memory, otherwise you would get lost. We always found our way, as long as we went on automatic, using our natural senses.

It was August about, and after a long walk in the night, we somehow reached the path left of the first bridge and the old mill. After a short while, we climbed up onto a path which went through the olive groves and then, we climbed down to the river stream. This is where you had to take off your shoes and roll up your jeans, stepping from stone to stepping stone, by boulders and trees. I collected my gear, which I had hidden, and continued behind Mona, up the river, until she said jovially, "We're home!" Bending under some trees, I came out into an open area with a sandy clearing, a pool and the sound of my first waterfall! She lit a candle on a rock and I helped her build a fire. Shortly, I could smell something cooking, as she offered me one of her Ouzo-teas. We ate and talked and I knew that we would make love, Mona had decided so and the wine helped. We got into our bags, as the sky cleared into a heaven full of stars, and we said how beautiful it all was. How, down here by the riverbed, the water and sounds of nature stirred our emotions and feelings. I kissed her and touched her back, and she let me make love to her. In life, she was not to be dominated, but in love-making, she liked to lie back in a helpless way, and scream and sigh with ecstasy like pain and she sighed a lot! I half knelt, with my legs outside her thighs, with which she gripped me and I rode her, like one would some kind of animal, and imagined, she imagined that I was a satyre and she a nymph. Her screams always frightened me, but she said that she enjoyed herself, and sometimes in the middle of the night, I would wake up to the sound of her sighing like a wild female creature. In Athens, I saw little erotic statuettes of such half-humans and one a beautiful female, except for a male part! Was Mona trying to be like this? We fell into a long sleep and woke up late, for we didn't have the correct time. We made breakfast, amid sun drenched flowers and trees, rivercrabs, waterfalls and pools. Then we went under the waterfall to shower togeth

The Mill

The Grotto by the river.

pressures, things were possible! She lay on a large boulder to dry, and I on another, but not together, like a traditional couple. I felt the urge to make love to her, but she wouldn't allow me.

I said to her "Look! It's hard! and she laughed, "Nature again!" and she jested at my genuine surprise.

She disappeared up the river and I waited. When she didn't return, I left and made my way to the hill-top where I could see the mill, the valley; but not the river, for it was completely hidden from view. There, I painted, and the buzzing sound with the wind blowing my sketchbook, made my art strenuous and difficult. Sometimes, I would throw a rock at the trees, but shortly, the buzzing would continue, and the heat was too much for painting, I was sweating profusely and the scene had so many variations, that it was easy to lose the symbolic meaning. After a few hours like this, I went down the goat-path to Plakias for a swim and a coffee and bumped into Mona. We had a word and then she went off again. I sat in the fish restaurant and drew the tables and 'lip chairs' and the trees, moving with the sea breeze. Then I took a walk on the beach, away from the fish restaurant, towards Cape Stavros, beyond which, was a long yellowish beach. After a long walk, I decided to go for a drink before it got dark. I went into one of the disco-bars, called 'Vulgan' and ordered a bottle of red wine, and knew that I would get soaked. By 9 o' clock I was. I somehow, made my way in the dark, several times, falling down on the prickly bushes, but I was in a great mood, and still conscious of what I was doing. Only, my bodily co-ordination didn't seem to respond to my commands. After a long time, I came close to Mona's camp and I could see her fire as she whistled! She was glad to see me, and I kept saying to her "You're artistic, beautiful and intelligent" repeatedly.

I went to bed and fell into a drunken slumber. When I awoke, Mona was in a good mood, and I wanted her. She refused, but I forced her and she let me. She felt sticky and sad which turned me on. Then, she was unhappy, because I was unpleasant to her and it took all afternoon for her to recover. Then we walked into Plakias together and she cheered up. I felt guilty, but satisfied. We had a good meal, and sat in our usual bar, talking. When we got back to the river, everything was fine again. Mona "Last night you kept saying to me". I interrupted her, 'I know, you're artistic, beautiful and intelligent'. The rest of the day we spent down by the river like Adam and Eve.

117

A funny scene

I am cooking over an open-fire and Mona is lying nearby, naked and asleep with after-glow. Suddenly, I see a pair of hairy legs below, in front of me. I carry on cooking, believing them to be an apparition, without looking up. Slowly, I raise my eyes, and there before me, is a naked Greek man, with black hair, in his twenties, crouching down and bent kneed-to speak to me. I act casual, as if all is normal, and he says "This is a private place!" From this I gather that we are squatting on his hidden lovenest, to where he takes his tourist girls! "Have you found a knife and sleeping-mat?" he asks. "Yes" I reply, with a friendly smile. He doesn't seem angry and grins. "We will leave them, when we leave this place" I added.

"Drop in for a drink on the house, at my taverna!" he says.
"Sure, we will" I answer, thanking him for his offer, "Thanks!"
"Goodbye!" he gestures with his hand, as he moves off along the river bed and trees in a Tarzan like manner, skillfully, with leaps and bounds!
"See you!" I wave to him.
"Don't forget the drink!" he concludes, as he disappears into the bush. Through all this, Mona doesn't wake up. Later I describe the funny scene to her. The man is the waiter-owner from our regular cafe, he is from the mainland, and quite different from the locals.

That evening we stayed by the river, and when she was cooking I asked her; "Where did you go this morning? "I waited for you, after you went up the river!" "I was worried about you!"
"Oh, I went swimming and then I did my painting."
"I thought that you were having a river orgasm!" I added.
"I didn't think you knew my secret!" she smiled.
"Oh yes", I told her "I guessed at it, sorry!"
"It's alright"

Another Incident

After dinner when Ingar was dozing on the sands by the pool, I had an impulse. She was reclining in the shade, displaying a beautiful ginger Mount of Venus, with her breasts sloaping downwards. I mixed some acrylicpaints, and drew with my brush, painted tattoos on her face, and rings of colour, in arabesque, around her breasts, with circles around her nipples and red on her teats. She woke up with the tickling of the brush-hair, looked along at the body-painting-and laughed. I designed it so that the breasts were in the shape of a scrotum, coming down in a marrow shape, to form a tip at the point of her belly button. Then, I painted her legs and arms to outline her bones in a skeleton design. I asked her to stand in the bush on a boulder, with the sun shining behind her, and to hold a long bamboo rod, like a spear. She looked like an Indian. Afterwards we both went under the fall, flirting and the paint flowed away.

"I want to be Mona"

Body-painting

The Tap-Shop

Slowly, I was falling in love with Mona, though I told myself, that I would not! She, however, was trying to keep a certain distance between us. I reminded her of the waiters offer and we took it up! He was very friendly, and not at all a money-grabber! That evening, I said to Mona, that it was time for me to go back and see Nikos and get my suitcase, which was full of paints and paintings and drawings. I couldn't lose them. I also owed him some money. I was missing Stavros, the village, and the taverna and Nikos's company, and its special atmosphere.

We rose early that morning, and Mona was now relaxed and opened up. She was tanned and she looked happy, and so was I. We went down to the river, carrying our shoes and other daily items in a small rucksack. When we got to the riverbank, we put on our shoes and strolled along to the first bridge and the tall mill. Mona was wearing a long striped dress and earrings, her hair was short and she looked good. She stopped for a moment, picked a green olive, burst it and rubbed the oil on her lips. "It's good!" she said to me "Try some!" I did. A blue bird whistled in a tree, as we crossed the bridge, and made our way up along the path, past the prickly pears and grapevines growing in and around the mill. I could just make out the water-trough going along the hillside, where it used to, in years past, flow down to the top of the mill and then fall and turn the grinding wheel. It was a long steep walk, and she picked herbal flowers for tea. Mona knew them all and she could tell the various scents and smells. Eventually, we came to the winding road by the war-memorial and just past the small empty church. I anticipated problems at Nikos's but I felt that I was in the right, and when I told her of my anger at the Dutchman, she said "You must change your bad feelings into creative ones!" I knew that she was right, still, it wasn't that easy because anger can eat you up, when you take it into yourself, which I imagined, a Cretan would never do! But she had done a lot to help me! We got to Stavros and it was early afternoon and silent. Nikos was sitting inside, and I wondered what he would say. The Dutchman saw me from the balcony, and his face almost caved in, like I was going to get my revenge!

I thought that I better face the music, whatever it was! I went upstairs to the hostel bunk-rooms, and looked for my case. It was gone! I asked the Dutchman. He said Nikos had it because he thought that I had left without paying, or I wasn't coming back! I went down to the taverna and saw Nikos and said "Is everything okay, my case has gone?" "Yes, everythings okay - no problem!" But he was angry with me, or himself. I told him how I had been waiting for a cheque from home, and that I had been waiting to pay him. He got the suitcase and threw it along the taverna floor at me, with anger, yet with friendship! "Theres's nothing in your suitcase I would want! Why would I take it?"

I was happy to have my drawings and paintings back, and more than happy that Nikos was still my friend! That evening, we went to Nikos's to eat and drink, I was nervous but soon the wine quelled my fears, and anyway, Mona had her arm around my shoulder, as if she really liked me, as she talked to a bearded man, and Nikos was happy for me and said admiringly, "Where did you find this one? Mr. Picasso!" "Mr. Picasso is back!" he said, smiling and directing his words at the Dutch couple, and I knew he had sussed them out! It was then that evening, that I realized how beautiful Mona really was. You see, she had, up to that time, been dressed in hiking gear, with her hair cut short. As we walked back down the goatpath to the mill my torch shone on her back. Her dress was furled at her waist, and the light illuminated her curved shape. She had a fair face and a sensitive intelligence. The moon was out again and tomorrow we would go and visit the Holy Grotto, down there, beyond the mill. She was really a lady of mind and spirit, and she just wanted to be herself! I looked at her face and she said "I want to be Mona!"

Adam and Eve and the mythical gods and goddesses in the landscape

Time passed and we became part of the river, living like noble savages, not really real primitives, or aboriginals, for we were not in any danger, more like the "Free life naturists" and after a while, we didn't feel unconventional or abnormal in any way, there was only Mother Nature and us. We were like castaways in a safe place, and not far from civilisation. In this 'natural' environment, it was easy to see the Satyres and Nymphs and other Gods and Goddesses, and apparitions come out of the trees! I never ventured much further up the river, from where we were camped and there was so much I had left undiscovered. That particular morning, Mona took me to see the Holy Grotto. It was somewhere near the first mill, a little white house built into the cliff face, and surrounded by trees. I approached the place with respect, for I was a believer, though I felt that Mona wasn't religious, despite her love of nature and her tinkering with Animism. Despite her love of beauty and art, (she had a desire for female emancipation), and awe at the sight of those Icons of the Virgin-Mother, and even in spite of her wanting the return of the female Goddesses to their rightful place; Mother Earth and Aphrodite! There was a calm, pastoral atmosphere around the Grotto, like one of those medieval paintings. It had a small lattice window, with flowers in a vase. Walking up towards it, among the olive groves, it was easy to believe in miracles and saints, away from the influences of the materialistic City. Inside, were various offerings and requests for divine or saintly intercession. I crossed my fingers on my leg as a sign of belief and respect, and later that day, I went up the path to the mill and drew it from up high. From there, I could see the Grotto below, and the valley stretching along into Plakias, and beyond, the blue sea and blue sky, and to the right of me, the Gorge, covered with olive trees and hills. Where did the river go, I wondered? I left Mona painting, near the power station, she was doing a water-colour of Stavros, up there on the hillside. Later, we compared paintings, and she remarked how different our inpressions were, of the same place! It was about this time, that I started to do my Greek cigarette packet drawings, inside each packet, was a nice white virgin, rectangle of card, which was excellen for fine drawing with a HB pencil! That evening Mona invited me for a meal, not to Nikos's but to the Tap Shop, which was just up the road from the hostel pub. She felt that there was something bad about Nikos's, and I told her, how it must have changed since I left. But I said that it would change again! We walked up the path by the mill and this was always a refreshing stroll, before what was bound to be a good night! She was wearing her long dress, as was her liking, and we had become good friends! At the end of the path, it would bend into the open, and when there was a strong wind, it could be danger-ous. We walked down the road, past the war memorial, the stream by Wolfgang's house and entered the Tap Shop, where we sat at a table on the balcony. Mona sat in front of a large plant, with her ear-rings dangling and I drew her! I was in love with her! From the balcony you could see the whole bay, with the two capes, Plakias and the sea, with the sun setting and the moon very faintly coming to life! We ate and drank and talked, and soon the taverna was full of young holiday-makers in groups, always in groups. Mona said "Tomorrow, we must go to Rete, I must get more money!" "So must I" I added. "Then I can stay four more days before going to the Peloponesse!" Maybe another week with Mona and then I would be alone - I thought to myself, and drank back a gulp of wine, but at least it was a reprieve. "I must go to a place past Hania and get a boat" she informed me. I pretended not to hear, as I didn't want to! I couldn't get it into my head that there was going to be an end to our relationship and our adventure.Would I ever see her again? She seemed so logical about the whole thing, sen-sible and accepting what must be, or fulfilling her plan? For now, she was my lover and friend and I longed for it to continue.

Tomorrow, the only thing which would worry me, would be the bus journey along the Kotsifou-Gorge, and wondering if I would ever get to Rete alive! I would try to have an argument with Mona, saying "I'm not an experiment! Don't you have any feelings?" "Can you just forget everything that's happened to us?" "It's the same for me. It would be alright if we both lived in the same town. Anyway, back there, it would be different! We would be different people!" "Of Course, Brendan, I care!" She'd say sincerely.

But I thought, in my emotional way, that she was too Teutonic and rational, like other friends of mine from those countries in the North of Europe. So we went to Rete, and I took here to the Souvlaki taverna. After the bank we sat there and I gave her a pair of Cerulean blue worry beads, as a token of my love, and I thought that she didn't yet in her life realise how precious love was, and she shouldn't miss its chance! But she didn't want to fall in love, and she asked if I had intended them for Vannila! It was strange how my feelings had changed towards her. Those first few days we were good friends, and now, I wanted more. If only I could go back and start again, but there in the Tap Shop everything was perfect, and I had everything I could desire. We sat on the balcony all evening and drank lots of wine, and discussed Life and Art and told funny stories; "Have you heard about the Irish dog with three legs, eating a bone by the fire?" Mona smiled with her first taste of Irish humour. Then I started to tell her a joke an Australian told me in Nikos's.

Inside the taverna, four old men are playing cards and Cretan music plays. "Have you read Jung?" I asked her, "You know! About Anima and Animus!" "Oh yes Anima, the male side of the woman, and Animus the female side of the man!" We were in perfect tune. She sits under a large green rubberplant. I say, "If the male part of the woman fits with the female part of the man, then there is a good harmonious relationship and vice versa. "You mean, that we are Hermaphrodite-half-man and half-woman?" "No" I say, "Not at all". She still thinks in 'Bisexual' terms. "No, I mean like, Ying and Yang!" Then Mona realizes what I mean. "Yes, that right!" and we, simultaneously, come to the same conclusion. Like a puzzle suddenly solved! Mona's striped dress, the plant, her ear-rings, the taverna, the moon and the whole atmosphere, flow in arabesque into each other with my feelings of Stavros. And all the good friends I had met there. I even felt, in a sentimental way, homesick for Hibernia, and the holy ground, I longed to kiss. The Cretan music broke my heart, as Mona would, She was my muse, and soon to take flight. And Michaelangelo's words haunted me, that beautiful night, amist all my happiness.

"Don't be a victim, Brendan. Don't be a victim!"

We walked back down the path past the Mill and I observed her bottom again and smiled to myself. The moon was bright and lit up the whole valley... We made this trip several times, and I spent my days drawing and painting and all was well with us, until our last night near Stavros. When we went to bed, I wanted to make love to her but she refused me and at about 3 am that night, it started to rain. It was a Monsoon of a shower, and the trees and bushes dripped (as in the Tropical-Rain-Forest?) We moved our stuff into the cave but the rain blew in. So we decided to leave for the Grotto, for better shelter. I was going to leave my suitcase and rubbish in the cave and she told me off. I complained "Then what? Can I do with it? It's too much to carry?" And she replied "What do you think the river can do with it?" She was right, the winter floods brought all the tourist rubbish down the streams and river and it was caught by rocks and trees and visible in the summer shallows. We decided to go down the river to the Grotto, for shelter. It was the middle of the night, as we waded and tiptoed through water and along the stones. I still persisted with her, as we took off our wet clothes, but she wasn't having any. Later, she relieved me and I said "I would do it for you!" The wine had made me depressed, as I was already sad to leave the river, but Mona was resigned to the fact! She said accusingly "But I thought you said that you wouldn't ever sleep in the Grotto. Now you want to make love there!" "Yes" I said, with mixed feelings and signs of guilt. We packed and went down to Plakias to catch the bus to Rete, but first we had some Nescafe-coffee. We both agreed, that it tasted fantastic.

The Pebble beach at Plakias.

Hania and departure

We sat outside the bus-stop cafe and waited. Mona talked of her art-work back in Bremen Art-School and I envied her having something to go back to! Soon, we were on the bus, and in moments, turning around at Stavros and having a last look (I thought that I would never see the place again!) Then around the bends in Kotsifu Gorge and into Rete. Having an Ouzo on the seafront of Rethymenon and catching the bus to Hania. The hustle and bustle of the bus-station, back packers on their way to Stavros, Plakias and other places, arrivals and departures, villagers on their way home, and me, into the unknown. We came to Hania, at last, where there was a large festival taking place. I had passed the Bay of Suda and the harbour from where I could have caught my boat, but when the bus stopped briefly there, I declined to get-off (and Mona said nothing at all, as if she were asleep to things). I continued into Hania with her. We had a beer, and I said that I would stay with her that night, until she caught her bus to Kastelli for the boat to the Peloponnes. She said to me "I am in a strange mood!" admitting "I have found my Phantasie of Kreta!" (Her foreign accent was clear, and it was, romance to my ears, deep and soft). "I have found my dream! and now I am happy to be going to the Peloponnes and at the same time unhappy to be leaving you, Brendan." We had stretched our time to its limit, and I had to go back via Athens, so this was our last night together! We strolled down to Hania Harbour, and there were hundreds upon hundreds of Greek families at rows and rows of tables, eating and drinking and enjoying the dayoff. It was No Day, when the Greeks had said No to Mussolini. There were large crowds gathered and speakers preaching against Nuclear Weapons, and even the waiters wore CND badges! The Harbour was lit up and the atmosphere was electric. There are always new things to be had in Crete, even when you are saying Goodbye to your best friend! We enjoyed this interlude, and later we walked back throught Hania to the bus-station, where we slept, while she waited for the early bus, she wanted to make love that night, but we had nowhere to do so, and she said, "How strange! when you wanted to Brendan, I didn't!" When the bus came she smiled and I stood sleepy, rigid and stiff, unable to

Chapel of Timios Stavros - Lefkoyia.

Bapma

smile and kiss her goodbye.

Mona hugged me, and said "Look at you!" smiling at me as I stood rock-like. I waited all day for the boat, alone and depressed, and when at last, we were seabound out of Suda Bay, I looked back at Crete and I thought that I would never see it, or Mona again! And how wrong I was.

Part Three

Coming Home! The Life of Reilly!

I had arrived home at last after a long arduous journey South, to the Sun, and my adopted village. I came from a Mediterranean island off the shores of Northern Europe, left of Britain. It had all the characteristics of a typical Mediterranean place, island, dancing, singing, poetry, good conversation, eastern music, and the Crack, lacking only the sun's strong rays. As I passed the door of the Taverna, to deposit my bags upstairs I heard Moma's voice "Brendans back, Nikos!" Within minutes, I was sitting on a stool at the bar. It was mid-afternoon, and I was holding a big lager, and smiling at Nikos. He gave me a short on the house, and said kindly "Relax, Brendan!" This was the only place I had ever been where I didn't wish to be anywhere else! The Cape was out there in the sea, and I was content to wait and bide my time, for whatever might happen, conversation with the villagers, or with travellers like myself. Romance, Art? All I needed was time, time to savour the joys and secrets of this, the Good-Place, meet my true-love, discover the source of the river, and find the village of Irish builders-of-Venetian-boats! And that was not much to ask, or was it? In fact, at that moment, I wasn't searching for anything! I knew that I had arrived, and I would leave the rest to fate. I ate a big meal of chops, drank some more frothy beer, and fell asleep upstairs, for the rest of the afternoon.

When I came down later that evening (after a cold shower), I sat at the bar again. The taverna was quiet, with a few people sitting at tables. At the table behind me were three women, an attractive blonde, slim and shy, a mysterious brunette, and a short-haired woman with a friendly smile. I said 'Hello' to them, but only the short-haired woman was responsive, because her English was good and the other two were too embarrassed to converse, with their limited vocabulary. The woman with the dark brown hair, looked angelic and fanciful and deliberately let her long hair fall down over her face, to hide a

Mama Plakias. 31 st August '85.

beautiful but serious countenance. She wore a white cotton summer dress, while her friends wore jeans. She was the more feminine of the three but she was, however, totally unapproachable and lost in some kind of dream; capricious and reserved, as if she was above everything. The blonde woman looked to me, to be Scandinavian and the petite woman could have been German. I sat at the bar and told them, that I had just arrived and apologised for my having interrupted them. Then, I turned back to the bar and Nikos. The paintings were still on the wall, and the old place hadn't changed that much.

I was on top of the world, and I had said to an Irishman in London, telling him of my discoveries, that one day I would get back to the village, and be sitting there at the bar again, looking out at the bay! So it was possible to make your dreams come true, as the Dutch-Indian man had said to me on the boat, "Life is a series of hurdles!"

Next day, I recuperated, walked about the village and sat in the sun outside the taverna, only one time going down the donkey-path to Plakias beach and not daring to go to the river. Anyway, the atmosphere was completely different, as if a new chapter had begun. It was always changing in Stavros. I mean, in the taverna, new faces and new people and auras. Nikos was constant, the corner-shop, the post-office, the chairs and tables on the other side of the street, overlooking the bay; the clothesline and plants on the hostel-wall, were all there! It was still possible for me to come back as I had never really "blown it" here! The lamp-post was there, but the dog was gone. In the taverna, a party of locals were devouring a pot of rabbit stew, just for the sheer fun of it. It was getting near supper-time, so I shaved and had another shower. I would make my first week here, a holiday, after that, start some serious drawing and painting, and maybe later, find a job. On my way back to my bunk, I accidently went into the wrong room, where the blonde woman was combing her long shiny hair (she was naked but for briefs). I said "Sorry" and she smiled, as I hurriedly made my exit! I went downstairs and sat at a table and devoured some of Moma's meatballs and chips, with a glass of red village wine. Then I sat at the bar and sipped an ouzo, with the mandatory glass of water. I was happy and content and seeking nothing and no-one. The blonde came and sat outside by the open window. She had a small red and blue Indians-feather in her hair, and she was looking away from me at the sky and the moon. It was very quiet, while I sat there, only speaking to Jim, the painter and decorator who was here again. I said to him that I had the strangest feeling that the blonde woman liked me! But how were there such vibrations? I had hardly spoken to her and then she was stand-offish and reserved. After about an hour, I had a feeling that she was aware of my presence at the bar even though she didn't for a second, turn around and look at me. All I noticed was her hair and the feather and a definite image of her face, which was planted in my mind by that first meeting. The face was, in a way, very familiar but we had never met before in our whole lives. All this time, which seemed to last forever, I could feel intuitively, her almost imprerceptable female vibrations, urging my curiosity and provoking my male instincts. I knew that this was a kind of unspoken invitation and that my chance would soon slip away, if I didn't take the plunge! Something beyond my control was pushing me out the door, and before I knew what I had done, I was sitting next to her at the table out-

Susanne at Damnoni-Taverna.

Susanne & me playing by the rocks at Cape Kakomouri.

side, and saying "What a beautiful night it is!" I heard myself say to her "Would you like to make a walk?" She stood up, almost immediately, and as we walked away from the taverna, I saw the English couple wave at us. The road was dark and the moon full, and she kept saying "Schön, schön, schön", Beautiful, beautiful, beautiful. We embraced, about halfway up the road, and kissed. I caressed her bosom and we walked, hand-in-hand back to the taverna. We talked and later, I bid her goodnight, lay on my bed and went into the softest, deepest sleep I had ever had in my whole life. That was the effect she had on me. Susanne, my opposite, my twin!

I remembered the boat journey across the water to Crete, landing at Hania, the bus to Rete, the bus to Stavros, but the boat part, was the best. The atmosphere was full of interest and excitement, meeting new people and full of expectation. The fresh food, the air of friendliness, that only the Greeks can create, being all together, and everyone having a say, and a place, people merging into groups.

As in my own country, one could talk to strangers but there were really no strangers in Greece! We were all a family! There was even a chapel on the mezzanine, and on the top deck, I fell asleep as secure as a babe in arms, looking up at the clear starry sky and listening to the hearbeat of the ships engines and the gushing of the seawaves as the ship ploughed its way through the flat moonlit ocean. Then the landing on Crete. There was nothing much there at the harbour, but my feeling was not of going and ending but of coming and beginning. It's almost as if I were arriving at a predestined time, a few days either way, and everything would have been utterly different. I knew, that I had arrived in Stavros at the right time and I was at the right place, with the right person, on that fateful night!

The next day, Susanne went with her lilo to Damnoni-Beach and was accompanied by the two other women. I waved them goodbye and said that I would see them later after I had done some drawing. I walked down past the Shell station and beyond where I found a suitable spot in which there were some beautifully formed olive trees, with plastic nets, black and stretched across the ground, held down by grey rocks, with some patches of green grass sticking through. I sat under a tree and decided to do an acrylic painting on paper, which I did, slowly, until I was satisfied that it was completed. I got the view and effect, that I wanted and as it was getting hot, I decided to carry on to Damnoni to have a swim and see Susanne, the one I liked. When I got to the beach, Damnoni taverna was busy and full of bronzed-skinned people. I got myself a lemonade and sat down and looked around for Susanne at the tables, amid the trees. She was nowhere to be seen and so I wanderd along the beach, on which there were luscious, suntanned nudes. In the distance I could see Susanne waving! I walked over, wearing a cap and sunshades, and looking like an American tourist. The brunette and the petite woman both smiled in a formal manner.They were bare-breasted and attractive. One-by-one they said their goodbyes and tactfully made their exits from the scene. Later, we all met by the trees in the taverna, and I did a drawing, cartoon-like in style, of Susanne, windswept with the chairs, sun and sea. She was amused and we were soon the best of friends. We were full of each other and we both assumed that the other, was rich or famous. It was a beautiful sunny day with the smell of sea and salt, like the kind

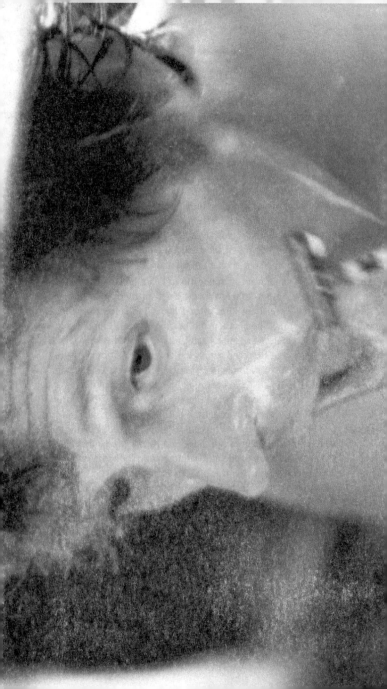

of holiday, people in the city dreamed of. The sky was clear and the waters along the shore were cerulean blue with dashes of emerald. For the woman, it had all the natural ingredients to make her attractive, for the man, there was a constant display of female shapes and intimate views.

When I was swimming by some rocks, I came near to the beach, where there were two naked girls kissing on the sand. All around was the sunny island landscape and various titillations by the seaside. Susanne and I were lucky, in the sense that we were not just seeking physical pleasure but we were fascinated by the beauty and romance of Crete, with its harsh edge! The three women got a lift back to the village (girls could always get lifts!) and I walked up the winding road, looking up at the deserted cottage on the top of that hill, which overlooked Stavros. When I got back to the hostel, the big Dutchman was shaving and talking to Susanne. She went into her room and I sat on the balcony and admired the view. I had met the big Dutchman before, on my last trip, and he loved the place, as I did myself. I said to him "Oh, just look at it," looking out at the cape and sea. And he said in his soft way "Bootiful place, bootiful place!" After I had cleaned up, we both went downstairs to eat. He was a kind, soft man from Holland, and one Christmas later, he sent me a photograph of me shaving. Susanne came and joined us as we ate delicious Lamb Kebabs and dipped into the Greek salad with fresh feta cheese and sipped the red village wine. She returned to her friends, while I talked with him. Susanne told me later, that he thought I was a great lover! It made me laugh, his exaggerated impression of me! That night we all sat at a long table, drinking and telling stories and enjoying the company of people from other countries, while the Greeks carried on their social-life in separate (though not hostile) way. Later, I sat outside with Susanne and around midnight, we went for a walk up past the war-memorial and around the bend by some small patches of grass. At this point in our friendship, I thought that she was a business woman. The moon was out, as we embraced. "Do you want to make love?" I said, as I fondled her responding breasts under an embroidered thin white blouse. "Yes" she said softly. She made me feel manly and I behaved well and caressed her skilfully with tenderness and affection. She lay on the sun burnt grass and bending over her I stroked her reciprocating face-cheeks, nose, mouth, swaying my goosepimpled self along her long blonde hair and cheeks and lips. As

Me shaving on the Hostel roof.   137

I was about to make love to her, she said (I misunderstood her) "My children, my children". She had, in fact said "Use something, I want no children". All this happened in a flash and I said "It will be better tomorrow, I promise you".

We walked back arm-in-arm to the taverna. It was the most romatic setting one could imagine and nothing could have gone wrong because we were, from the first, good friends! From that moment when I saw her sitting outside the taverna, with her feather, as if she had been waiting for me all along, as if we both had come at an appointed time to this spot, to a prearranged meeting, with someone who was at that precise time crossing our love-line. And this someone we unwittingly, already knew, a kind of Karma. It was now late, and we ascended the spiral stairway to the bunks on the roof. We lay cuddled together on my bunk outside, looking at the sky, talking in a secret and friendly, intimate way, so surprised at finding each other. I wanted her to stay with me, but she needed to sleep alone for some reason of her own. So she went and I fell asleep happy to be awakened by the sound of music, blaring out from the loud-speaker of the chair-van and later the vegetables-lorry and the women nattering, as they bid for fresh vegetables. I looked down, with bleary eyes, at the scene below and the lovely view. Granny was watering the plants, the Dutchman was shaving at the mirror and he said "Good morning, Brendan". Susanne was brushing her hair. I smiled and said "Good morning". Soon after, I boiled some eggs and we sat outside at the balcony table, eating breakfast in an unhurried well mannered way. "Would you like to come with me to the river today?" I asked Susanne. "Oh yes, I would love to see it!" She smiled in her flirting, girlish way. I had told her of the pools and waterfalls and I thought, how good it would be to be alone with her. So, we bought some cheese and bread and chocolates from Moma, below in the taverna kitchen. She was peeling vegetables and greeted us "Kalimera, Brendan, Kalimera Susanne!" We both replied respectfully "Kalimera, Moma!" She had a big, naughty smile... Then we had a coffee and greeted various people, who were going to the beach, and set off for the path up the road. Nikos saw us and shouted suggestively "Mr. Picasso, where are you going?" I waved to him and grinned, as Moma served ice-cream to two middle-aged lady tourists.

I led the way, as I was the guide and explorer. We reached the path and strolled past the prickly pears and the small donkey field. The ochre grass was sunburnt and the way was clear and secluded by bushes. Susanne was care-free and had her hair tied up. She wore jeans and she looked strong and fit, slender and agile, with a nice way of smiling and getting her own way. But when she did, it was in the nicest of ways and she even had a kind way of being selfish. There was something basically decent about her, which I liked very much to the point of love. The language barrier wasn't a great problem as we were on the same wavelength! both emotionally and mentally. To me she was a good person, the light of my life, the apple of my eye!

We walked down and around the path towards the first mill, carefully making our way, and taking it all in, the various twists and bends, looking at the inside of the roofless rooms of the mill, smelling the herbs, touching the bushes and branches of trees, plucking the occasional olive, eating some fresh oranges and reading the shapes of the foliage, in all sorts of shades and penumbras.

We crossed the old bridge, stood for a while, to look at the flowing river, but unable to see up the stream, because of the trees and bushes. We carried along the hidden pathway by the stone wall and then, wading through the cool water, flowing from its secret source, we eventually reached the first waterfall, where we sat for a few minutes. There was no wind down here in the gorge, only a mild breeze, which now and then blew leaves across the clear waters, whereas, back on the hostel roof we would get the full measure of the winds from Africa. It was great to lie there, dozing or sleeping, with the gales screeching and howling outside. It got on some peoples nerves if it went on for many days, and they usually packed up and left for the north coast. If it got too bad, everyone would be in a bad mood. But the wind saved the valley from complete commercialisation, and the lovely sunshine kept it busy enough.

"Come" said Susanne, breaking my thoughts.

"Okay, I'm coming now!", I replied. She was keen to see more of the concealed riverway and try some of its natural delights. When we reached the second waterfall we swam in the deep pool and stood under the torrent of ice-cold water, then sat and lay on some long flat boulders to dry and laze about in the warm sun. All there was, was the sound of the water flowing, birds singing and our snoozing breath. It

139

Susanne by the river.

was rare to meet anyone down by the river, except the odd couple who managed to find their way down the hidden pathway, which went around and about the small Beehive farm. From the roadway, it was impossible to discern the pathline down in the bushes, if anyone found it, it was because they sighted the farmer, and as for the upper reaches of the river, they were completely unexplored! The bee-farm was fenced off and the farmer would usually frighten intruders away. The banks of the river were overgrown with tangled trees and bushes, carmine coloured flower plants and other vegetation, and nearby a large tree, was an enclosure of brambles and bushes with a sandy floor. It was getting too hot.

So I invited her over there to rest. I laid a mat on the ground in the Den, and we lay naked, side by side. After a silent time, Susanne stroked my leg with her toes. I turned and kissed her, in response to her initiatory caress, and when I began to rush things she said instructively, "Relax, slowly! Brendan" She liked my smell. It was wonderful to be alone with her and making love, with only nature around us. She taught me how to relax and take things easy.

For the first time I was completely unwound, and it all happened so soon after my arrival in the village. After a timeless period, we walked back downstream. Susanne was leading they way, and I noticed how wide her shoulders were and how she had a natural catwalk. She was born poor but she had an aristocratic poise, with a proud bearing, and she had done it all herself. She was sophisticated and good-looking, a bit wild, and determined to be self-sufficient. By the grotto, I picked some olives and rubbed some of the oil on her lips and gave her a good hug. Then I showed her the inside of the shrine, and she said "Beautiful" softly. It was all new to her and I wished to show her nice things, and she seemed to like the same things as me. We returned over the bridge, around the mill, and up along the donkey path to the war memorial and the village . When the wind was strong, it was impossible to go down the path, or around the bend in the road to the gorge. But the motorcars did it and some went over the side, you could see the little shrines at the roadside. My plan had been to paint most of the time and then work, but now I was completely thrown over by Susanne, and I didn't want to lose her at any cost! Walking up to the Taverna, she turned to me and said informatively, "My manfriend is coming tonight on his motorbike!" At this time, I didn't really know much about her circumstances, or hadn't even thought about, whether she was single or free! Because we spoke different languages, sometimes there were little, (but important!) misunderstandings between us. "Manfriend!" Did this mean a friend or boy friend? And I didn't want to pry further, as I was prepared to be a winner. I was fit and confident, and I would not give her up to anybody, or for any reason. I would do anything and go anywhere to keep her, now that I had found her. Crete did the rest with it's happy times and long gregarious evenings, full of good company, characters and faces and celebration. And Nikos helping things along! When we got back to the hostel, we separated. I showered again, changed and lay on my bunk reading a guide to Crete, and relaxed in preparation for the evening ahead. The hostel was busy, with new arrivals, and the Australian manageress was polite and somewhat shy. She had lost

141

Imagination

all her money and so had to work to pay for her trip to England. She was lonely and kind.

In the kitchen, it was an Aussi scene, with a group of young men and women, but they were okay. Anyway, you meet all sorts, travelling and so it is better to keep an open mind, so that you can respond to people and learn about yourself. In Crete, you got to know yourself very well!

In the middle of our evening meal, the man on the motorbike arrived, he came to Nikos's, and Susanne greeted him in a demonstrative way, hugging and kissing him. She introduced us, and he seemed okay. His name was Peter, and he worked in a computer factory. He told me about Susanne's home, a big farmhouse in the country, and it sounded grand. He drew me a cartoon map of the place, in order to give me a good picture. He and Susanne were just good friends, and they had planned to meet up in Crete. The very next morning they left together on his motorbike on a day trip, and she was thrilled by the machine and the ravine roads. I went off drawing and that evening we all ate together. I passed her notes under the table, and she giggled at their contents, as I continued to invent cartoons, interweaving my time in the village with the life of Stavros. I bought her a huge cocktail, which Nikos decorated with flags, and the whole atmosphere was one of celebration and fun, with Nikos being the grand-host. He was happy that the place was busy and everyone was having a good time. A. Milne and his beautiful wife, sat watching the goings-on and later, I joined them to speak in English, and allow Susanne to converse in her own tongue. The Milnes were a retired English couple, and like me, Mr. Milne liked to paint. And I wished I could live in the village, as they did (Now I wanted Susanne to stay as well). The Milnes and I told stories and compared notes. They had come to the vilage on holiday, and one day decided, (They were in different rooms of their apartment) both thinking about the same thing; whether or not to come and live in the village? After ten minutes, they decided (without prior mention of the idea!) and coming together in the kitchen, they both uttered "Yes!" They stayed mainly for the sun, and from our first meeting, we got on really well, and of course, if I had been reasonably solvent, I would have stayed permanently, until I tired of paradise! I slipped Susanne a note again under the table, partly because I wasn't yet sure whether Peter had his eyes on her, and partly in fun.

143

The note said "Do you want to make a walk?" She read it, and nodded her head. She left first and later I did. I walked up the road towards the War-Memorial, and I heard her voice in the dark, "Brendan, here!" We embraced and I whispered in her ear "Love" and we walked under the moon as courting couples do, arm in arm. That day her girlfriend had gone on a trip to the Samari Gorge, and so we were alone in the bunk room. When we returned there, we lay on separate bunks and talked and looked out the door and over the wall, at the sky and stars shining. Sometimes we would go to sleep like that. But that night I kept making love to her. In the finish, she was bent over the bunk, I was being greedy, past all need. She would surrender herself to me, but it was no fun for her. Other times, we would sleep separately, and in the morning, she would come into my sleeping bag and sit astride me and I would submit to her. On our first night in a bunk together, on the roof we lay cuddled. I kissed the back of her neck and her ears, I faced her back and without a sound we joined together. We fell asleep in the dark and lay quiet to the wind and night sounds. She was good to me and it was all falling in love and getting to know each other.

After two days together, she went off on a trip to Matala up the coast. She and her friends, set off, I waved them goodbye and the bus drove away. I made an effort to spend the next days drawing and painting, as that was what I had originally intended to do, as least in the day time. But I had no studio, so I was compelled to work through the day. It was a fine routine-work all day, with coffee and swimming breaks and play at night. Anyway, I wasn't bothered with laying about in the sun all day. I preferred walking and exploring, drawing in the olive-groves and painting in the cool by the waterfalls. Often, I would paint, on the hostel roof, when everyone was out. I had plenty to do, and by now, I had conceived a partly complete picture of the village and its environs. But I wondered if I were seeing the place with tinted glasses arranging it for myself, into an ideal world. Michealangelo still shed new light on the history and origins of the place, and I desperately wanted him to show me the hidden caves over in the hills, and take me to Lower-Stavros towards Plakias. But he had to be in the right mood, before he would divulge his secrets! I had walked all over the cape and it's hills, looking for the lost village of Mirthios but had for the time being, given up the search. I spent my days painting and the evenings drawing, and thinking about Susanne.

Stavros

It seemed weeks since I had last seen her. Was it all just fantasy? or did she really like me, I didn't know, but I longed for her to come back. That morning, I woke and opened my eyes and standing over me was a nude woman, saying politely "Please, have you the time?" "Are you an artist?" She had seen my paints and brushes. "Yes", I moaned, with the sun blinding my bleary eyes. Then, the Mexican woman interrupted this naked doctor, and they disappeared into the backroom. The door swung open and I realised that I was missing a gorgeous sunny morning. I jumped up, and went for a shower and shave. The village was well into the day, and the locals must have thought us lazy, rich people, but really, our rucksacks were not full of money, as I thought they thought!

I ate one of Momas fried French toasts and drank herbal tea. For two days Susanne was away, I missed her and Nikos said "Whats the matter, Brendan?"

"Are you okay?"
"I'm waiting for my sweetheart" I sad, jestingly. "No problem!"

"She will return!" he said heartily, as he apron-clad, dried a plate in the kitchen.

"Brendan, where is Susanne?" Moma teased.

"Gone away with another man!" I said jokingly.

Moma laughed and Granny peeled the vegetables, she had just picked from their garden across the road. The sun shone outside and the rickety wooden table by the lamp post was empty. The night before, I had sat there eating dinner, and I had toppled off the chair, because of the uneven ground. Moma and the women all laughed, but I liked to clown about for them. The morning atmosphere was beautiful, with that glorious sun, not just a holiday feeling, but, everything was full of interest. You could just sit there outside and wait for someone to arrive or observe little happenings. Nikos made himself a large black coffee, and I sat outside with him. He was a tall man with huge hands. He worked all day, until late at night and into the morning. Moma never seemed to stop at all. I left Nikos for a swim at Damnoni and spent the rest of the day, painting under an olive-tree near the road to Plakias. I was happy and the picture was full of good feeling. The colour scheme and the composition were to my liking. The colours of Crete were coming into me and out into my pictures, and my dreams and prayers were being caught by those black nets. In a way, I was obsessed by the nets and up until now, I had never picked olives, or tried to earn a living here, so my vision was not marred by harsh realities. I could concentrate my mind and feelings on the beautiful side of life, with a touch of the arid and black, which gave Crete it's edge. On gravel ground men were building in the heat, mixing dusty lime and cement, their clothes and faces covered in white. I walked past them, to sit outside the fish restaurant, and watch the sea, or fish for squid from the rocky jetty. Later, sitting under on olive-tree, I studied the intricate shapes of the rocks and nets, and the various shapes and forms of the trees. I thought to myself that it was better not to work here at all, and instead enjoy the "romantic" side of things, otherwise my dreams and illusions would be diluted. Though these were (as a writer had said) creative illusions. Anyway, the nets did something for me. They suggested the sea and they were near the sea. I could have wrapped houses, cars, villages in those "dream nets!"

While I was at the bar getting some beers, Nikos asked me a question, "What does eccentric mean, Mr Brendan?" He was referring to the

English cyclist, who had stayed for a couple of days; and very often, these lone cyclists were indeed eccentric fellows. I explained to Nikos that the English cyclist was one, and the two Dutch hostel managers. And then Nikos further enlarged on the term, by saying "The English cyclist was a good eccentric and the Dutch managers were bad eccentrics! And Mr. Brendan is a good eccentric!" I recalled another bicycle incident. One day a Swedish girl had arrived, exhausted after cycling all the way down from Stockholm. She was obviously a keep fit fanatic, and she had one of those developed sports bodies from pumping iron; not the more grotesque, but rather she was of the Spartan maiden variety. For fear of thieves (but there were none) she kept her racing bike outside the bunkroom on the hostel roof. On the night before she departed, she was sleeping on a mattress outside near the bike. It was close, with a hot breeze blowing into the bedrooms, and I found it difficult to sleep. The moon was shining, as I leaned on the windowsill to refresh myself. As I took a deep breath, I could see her asleep, not far away from the window and the pink pebble-dashed wall. And then, unexpectedly, I hear the racing bike, with its ram-horned handle-bars, slide and gently fall from the wall onto the girls mattress. She didn't wake and I avoided looking at her pneumatic shape. Her legs were half spread eagled and coming to rest, the leather saddle seated itself under her frame, and then the pedals, after a slight half-turn of the chain wheel, stopped slowly at each of her feet; the straps slipping over her toes. For a moment there was silence, and then the pedal wheel made a slight turn, making her legs move with its motion. This occured several times, and then, the wheel and pedalling increased to a moderate speed. And as the chain turned and reached the point of pedal-effort, it hesitated and allowed her, still sleeping, to make a joint exertion, and the bicycle lights lit up with the power from the dynamo. Making the shape of the moon on the hostel balcony wall. Her hands moved and gripped her sleeping bag, behind her head, which she was using as a pillow, and she pedalled slowly and almost imperceptually. Her thigh muscles tightened and slacked and I thought that I was dreaming, so I returned to my sleep. Next morning, when I got up, I looked outside, but she had gone. All that remained was a mudguard, its rear reflector flashing in the sun.

That evening, I had a drink with the Dutch, punk-styled man. He had short, blonde, peroxided hair, and we had a continuous repartee and a particular sentence, which we would reiterate at the end of each con-

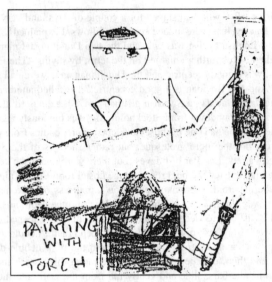

Cigarette Packet Drawings.

versation. He was divorced, and he couldn't get a job to suit his tastes in Amsterdam "Why can't you get a job?" I asked him. "It's the recession!" he replied. We both burst into laughter! I asked Nikos to put on some Irish music, like Paul Brady, Van Morrison or traditional fiddle music; or D. Kean, who had a sweet bird-like voice. The Dutchman liked Irish blues, but Nikos was often disinclined to play it, because he thought that most of his customers didn't care for the Irish stuff. He said that Irish music was either sad or for drinking; and not the kind you play all the time (like you could Greek). Other kinds of pop music was better for business, parties, eating, and drinking. So, he varied the music according to his mood, or the occassion, or to the needs of his clients. With great skill, he was spot on in his evaluations!

The next morning with a great sense of purpose, I jumped out of bed, did my various toilets and packed my painting gear, and rushed downstairs and had one of Moma's toasts and tea, and headed off, with my rucksack on my back, down the donkey-path to Plakias for a swim. I passed the first house at the top of the path, where a boy had slaughtered a pig and the blood flowed into the stream of water. There was always water (mostly soapy) of some kind flowing down here. There was also in this place, an interesting olive-tree with a rolled up olive net reclining over it's fork, in the shape of a rolled up carpet. I was getting to know a variety of olive-trees and nets, even after a years absence, I could remember them exactly. At the end of the first stretch of the path was a watering trough, a field of vegetables and some orange trees. I would always meet someone (sometimes a Greek and sometimes a tourist) coming up the track. I crossed over the dusty "road" and part of an irrigation stream. Usually, at this stage, it was very hot and I would take a drink of water from my bottle. On the last part of the track were a few houses, and a campingsite, then a bridge with bamboo trees and a sandy bit, with the occasional snake, where the road turned right to the power station. After swimming I did a painting of Stavros from the power station, up there in the hills, a fortress from bad-times. When I had finished, I had a cup of coffee in the fish restaurant, and watched the swimmers and fishermen. After a working day, I felt free to enjoy myself, and made my way up the donkey track. I thought of Marianna singing to herself "This is the dawning of...". It was a long, sweaty walk and I remembered how one of the Scot lads had run up it, rucksack and all! By the

149

time I got to the top, I was pouring with sweat, and almost staggered across the road to Nikos's bar. I asked for a lemonade from Nikos and as I gulped it back, he said to me, smiling "There's someone waiting to see you upstairs!" - I guessed at who it was.

I walked up the winding steps past the six toilets, along the balcony and past Granny's room. She was sitting talking to one of her old friends who was eightyfive but looked sixty! I went past the hostel office, where the Australian woman was at her desk, and into the bunkroom next door. I sat on my bed by the door, and I saw someone lying on the opposite bunk. I had come in out of the sun into the dark, so my vision was blurred, but I could just see some blonde hair and a face smiling and hear a voice saying "Hello" I recognised the shade of the blue around the neck! It was Susanne. We both sat there smiling at each other. I went over, kissed her on the cheek and then immediately sat back on my own bed. "Did you have a good time?" I asked her. "Yes!" she said. All I was interested in was that she was back. She was the most pleasant sight that I could imagine, all else was secondary, even painting! She was pleased to see me and she looked radiant. She wore a blue gypsy scarf around her neck and I called her the Blue-Bird after the bird we had seen by the river. (It had appeared out of nowhere and darted away upstream. I painted a picture of the second bridge across the river, on the path to Sellia, and in the middle of my canvas was the blue-bird).

Then, to my utter astonishment, I heard another familiar female voice coming from outside on the balcony! She was asking the Mexican woman "Have you seen the Irish artist, please?" I was flabbergasted and shaking with total surprise - IT WAS MONA'S VOICE! She came into the room, smiling at me and sat down next to me. She put her arm around my shoulders and gave me a hug. I gave her a reluctant one! I was nearly speechless. "How are you?" I asked in a withdrawn manner. "Fine" she said "I've been to Georgyioupolis and the lake. You don't know what I've been through" she said, surprised at my apparent disinterest. Then I uttered, "Susanne, she's my girlfriend and she's just come back now!" I was almost stuttering the words. "It's no problem!" she assured me.

I looked at Susanne and Mona alternatively. Mona said "Cool down!" "It's such a shock and surprise!" I said, "Come down to the Taverna and we'll have a drink, please!" The three of us went down to the bar

Carpet of Black Note

and sat at a table, I ordered some wine. I gulped it back and chain smoked. They spoke in a language, which I didn't understand so I couldn't explain to them both, in their tongue, and when I spoke to them in English, in which Mona was fluent, Susanne was left out. Mona's hair was slightly different, but she was, more or less, just as I had left her at Chania bus station that sad night! If only she had arrived on some different occasion and as she used to say - timing is most important with relationships. My rejection of her was unforgivable and she would never be my friend again! I had failed her and there would be no second chance! Mona was telling Susanne how we had lived down by the river together and I had thought, she had completely forgotten me! I had sent her a card before I left for Greece, but it was a long shot! And I guessed that if I had left two weeks later, that now, I might still be friends with, Lolita from the river!

Nikos watched the three of us from the bar and must have laughed to himself. Later, he joined us. Then everything relaxed. We ate and drank, and I left with Susanne. What a twist of fate! But I suppose I could never feel safe with Mona, after she had left me there in Hania, broken-hearted, I was afraid of what she could still do to me. They were both so cool!

Mona had come down from Turkey, then over to Crete, to Yeoryioupoli. She stayed by Lake Kournas, a fresh water lake, and she was exhausted after an incident with a guy; she had to take him to hospital after an accident. I didn't see much of her after that night and she had said to Susanne, that she was angry with me. She couldn't understand why I was so reticent and why I hadn't explained myself. Susanne and I went the next night to the Tap-Shop for a quiet meal, and while we sat at a table on the balcony, admiring the view, I saw Marianna! sitting (in an unusually quiet mood) with some odd fellow. She smiled and that was all! No more problems I wished to myself!

Susanne, said to me, probingly "You didn't tell me that you had taken someone else to the river!" "Mona said that you and her lived there last year!"

"Yes we did, Susanne, but you know that it was different with you!"

"Oh yes," she smiled, unconvinced and accussatively, "You probably take all your girls there!"

"No, No!" I replied "You know that you are very special to me, you know I Love you!" Then she said "You were very bad to Mona. She's upset. She can't understand why you were so unfriendly to her!" "I'll explain to her", I said. And then the subject was dropped as I added, "I promise!"

The next day Mona said goodbye and left for Lefkoyia; and now I had a problem with Susanne, she had to leave in two days, unless she could persuade her friends to go without her, and extend her air ticket. As I didn't want her to go so soon, I got Charles Henry to translate a note to her into her own language, and it said Blue-Bird don't go-Please stay! At dinner, the very next evening I passed it to her under the table. And she said "Yes, Yes, Yes, I'm going to stay! We have another week!"

For the next week we were together for most of the time, sometimes, down by the river, other times swimming at the beach west beyond Cape Stavros and the fish restaurant. The sun was too hot for me and I would lie under a bush, after a couple of hours sunbathing with her.

On the way back we would have a salad in the small restaurant before the bakery shop and drink a beer. A blonde woman, who was married to a Cretan man, served us and she looked as if she was working hard, child in arms and cooking in the heat. I knew her, and she had been many times to Nikos's visiting. One evening, a young French man sat near us and tried to chat up Susanne, I was steaming with jealousy. Nikos slammed the youth's drink down on the table, to let him know he wasn't welcome! Partly because, the hostel-girls were for the hostel-boys, so Nikos saw him as an interloper! (Susanne had said, she had been tempted, when she came upon the Frenchman at the river). Then one day, I had to take Susanne to the Airport to catch her flight to Berlin. We borrowed an alarm-clock from the big Dutchman, and got up early. We were amazed to find the moon still shining, and in the dark we got on an empty bus down to Plakias and there we discovered that it was only five in the morning! We had got up in the middle of the night! The big Dutchman had put his clock back 2 hours! We slept under an olive tree and I had a terrible hangover. It was Sunday morning, and I was unhappy even though I knew that I could see her again.

We had breakfast in a cafe behind Plakias front and everything was very quiet. Two middle-aged English ladies with Sunday hats and dresses approached us, and said "Excuse me, are you English, can

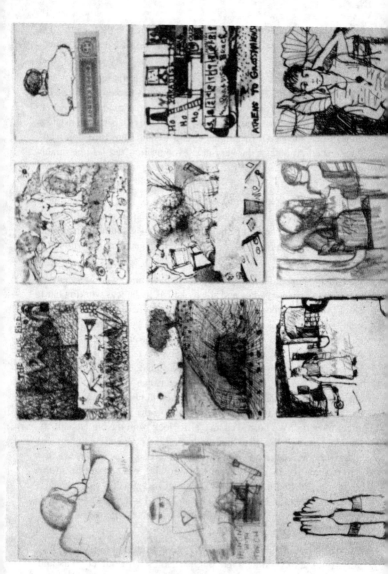

Cigarette-Packet drawing.

you please tell us where the nearest church is?" "We are Catholic and we want to attend Mass!"

I said "If you wait for the bus to Stavros, there's a chapel up there, I'm sure that they won't mind you going in if you wear scarves!" They went off, looking like some women from a Somerset Maugham short story, like old colonials, in flowery dresses.

We got the bus to Rethimno, then took another bus to Iraklion and then a taxi to the airport. We waited and waited and the whole affair dragged on. I just wanted to leave and get it over with. Susanne had a problem to persuade me to leave the village, I didn't want to go near, things like airports , supermarkers, town centres etc. Anyway, by the end of the day, Susanne wasn't allowed on a plane and the airport people told her to come back next week. She cried then, but only weeks later, when she returned to work, did she find that she had a week more of her holiday left! We returned to Stavros via Rete, where we spent one night on a top bunk in the close heat of a crowded hostel. We were next to each other looking out at the roof-tops and washinglines of Rethymnon and we were wakened by the noise form its busy streets. I took Susanne to the Souvlaki Cafe. The owners, two girls, and had grown somewhat since I had seen them last (and I was still unmarried!). In the Taverna, Susanne started a conversation with a young woman, who was sitting with a sixty year old man, I thought that they were Father and Daughter, but in fact they had just met travelling. They were both alone. He was Norwegian and she was Swiss and they had teamed up for a while. It was nice to see, in Crete the age gap didn't matter that much. We left the cafe and got on the bus for Plakias. Another week with Susanne and it was great to be going home. The bus passed Asomatos and I saw a crowd of bikers in black leather asking the way. I promised to stay in a hotel with Susanne for a few nights, partly for privacy and partly to try it out.

The next day, we booked into the Pension overlooking Damnoni beach. After a search we found a nice room with a double bed. We showered and were about to go out, when a terrible storm started. We could see the grey wild sea from the balcony. The wind blew fiercely, and we couldn't get out; it was too dangerous to walk along the road, you could be blown off the clifftop. We smoked and played on the bed. When it was sleep-time, she tried to move her part of the bed (the double was in fact two singles!) but I kept moving my part up to hers! She could only sleep alone! She felt trapped but anyway, the wind kept us awake all night! The Pension was so new that we could have been anywhere, Spain, France, anywhere! It was so easy to destroy the very things and qualities which attracted tourists.

It was about then that we both realised that the other wasn't rich! and money began to be a problem. But still, the sun always shone!

After a night in the Pension we decided to go to Lefkoyia, and I had wanted to go there for a specific reason! The storm was gone in the morning and we walked along the road by the olive-trees. Susanne looked good and I was happy to be with her. We made our way along the road to Lefkoyia, past bamboo and fig trees and oleander bushes and the various little houses. The village was picking up and going up market, places and tavernas were being done up. We came to the village, past the Tourist Pub and we walked up to the Partisan Cafe. Mona was sitting there! "Hello!" Susanne said, greeting Mona, in her high spirited way, "How are you going?" "Fine," replied Mona, as if distracted. "Sorry, I'm trying to make a phonecall and I cannot get through".

Out of context, I tried to explain to Mona why I had been unfriendly. I said "I'm sorry about my behaviour, but it was such a shock to see you again, and I couldn't explain to Susanne the situation, because she doesn't speak enough English. You two were talking together in your language, and I couldn't understand!" Mona wasn't really convinced and she was still hurt and felt uneasy and unforgiving. Susanne and Mona discussed the various ways (besides flying) of returning home. Bus, car, train. Then Mona cheered up. She said. "I must go now, see you later!" She left us and we went looking for a room, which we found. We bought some Feta cheese, bread, tomatoes and peaches from the minimarket. The room was white walled with a small kitchen and a tiny window; there was a double bed with white sheets and a blanket with red patterns. I can't say, how good the food tasted! It was fresh! It was simple and delicious. The colour and the taste was mouth-watering and our senses sharpened, making the foods we eat in Northen Europe seem like paper. We had the feeling there in that room of being away from everything. It was erotic being in a strange place, the whitewash, the dust, the rocking iron bed, the sleepy afternoon and the quiet. Susanne was being difficult, and said

Suzanne in the Pension near Damnoni Beach. ➤

she wasn't in the mood, so I forced myself on her. (She didn't seem to mind.) We spent the whole evening relaxing, reading and talking. Susanne was nice, but she could be very obstinate and spoilt. She would have her own way and be most charming about it!

In the morning, we went swimming at Damnoni. It was a long walk from Lefkoyia, but nevertheless, enjoyable. The sea was deep blue and Susanne's eyes were so blue from the sun. The light in Crete brightens up everything, and brings everything to life, the olives, the vines, the herbs, the pastel coloured flowers and even the rocky, dustry soil.

That evening we went for a meal in the Tourist Taverna and met Mona. She was in a much better mood and happy again. The three of us drank wine and watched the goings-on in the village. Sometimes, I would have a conversation in English with Mona and sometimes, she and Susanne would speak in their own tongue. Her hair was different, a bit shorter. I wondered that, if I could speak their language, whether I would see and know them in a different way? Then Mona said "I must leave you, I have been invited to a meal with a Greek family, they have offered me work on the Olives! They treat me like one of the family, See you tomorrow." She left, and we went to bed early and were in love again.

The next morning at breakfast we had a coffee with Mona, "They made me really drunk last night, giving me more and more wine and Raki, I got so drunk, but they wouldn't stop!" "I couldn't say no to their hospitality and they kept asking me to come and work on the olive harvest with them. It was a wonderful meal". Susanne said that Mona was going up to Stavros and we all caught the bus. It was full of travellers going to Plakias, and with that jolly Greek music, we felt as if we were just arriving. There was always that atmosphere on the buses at this time of year. When we got back to the hostel, we went to our bunks and Mona went on the roof (Most of what they said to each other I will never know!)

Susanne kept talking about going back home and I pretended not to hear. Her talk of leaving made me moody and it hit me, that she had her own, different life back home; whereas, I had buried my heart in Crete! That was the difference between the other visitors and me, I was never a tourist and I wanted to stay I went downstairs to the taverna into the kitchen, Moma was cooking and smiling. I asked her for some of her home-made yoghurt and she pointed to the fridge, explaining in Greek. I went behind the counter to get it. I opened what I believed to be the fridge, but I had opened the dishwasher! Moma shouted to Nikos (who was sitting at his desk by the door of the taverna) in Greek, laughing and telling him what I had done! He came around to the kitchen and the three of us started laughing. Things like this were hilarious here in the village. We returned to the bar and I had a small beer.

"Marianna has been looking for you, Brendan!" Nikos muttered.

"Oh, no!" I exclaimed, "You never know what she'll do next!" I finished my drink and said "See you." to Nikos. He returned to his accounts and I left. I walked down the donkey track. When I reached Plakias, I beachcombed along the sand towards Kakomouri Cape. I had a swim by the rocks near the peninsula. It wasn't deep and the weather was fine. I gathered my gear and made my way along the rocks as far as I could go, until I got a good view of the harbour, beach and valley. I sat and relaxed and made a watercolour. It was a lovely spot by the sea, with windsurfers gliding beyond the Cape. Later, I was joined by Susanne. I had been there with her a few days before, and we messed about in the pools in the rocks, like kids on holiday. Her hair blew in the breeze, and we lay on a boulder in the sun, with the smell of sea air and the waves gently lapping about. This was one of the best times we had together enjoying the simple things in life. We dozed off on my little reef that jutted up out of the sea. That evening we had a farewell drink at Nikos's and everybody had a good time. Charles Henry and his wife were there and the English couple and all kinds of people. One day an incoming wave carried him so fast, that he couldn't stop and he went hurling towards a reclining nude woman. As he fell onto her, she put her elbow up to protect herself! She broke two of his ribs! He had to go to the hospital in Crete.

As Nikos said many times "You could write a book about people who pass through here!" At one time there was a women's community living down the road. There were no other tourists or travellers about, so the taverna was packed full of women, most of whom preferred their own sex! For weeks and weeks, there was only Nikos and Michealangelo at the bar and fifty ladies sitting in the taverna! Nikos said "A customer is a customer. I will serve anyone who can pay!" But one day he had a scuffle with two of them and out of a bag fell an instrument of pleasure! It was funny to imagine Nikos and Michealangelo surrounded by unobtainable females! Bar a few disagreements, the villages would give everyone a fair chance to be free and easy.

The next day Susanne packed to leave for home, and she had made an arrangement to meet Mona at the Plakias bus stop. She had missed her flight, so she was going back by train. We said goodbye again, and she said her farewells to Moma and Nikos. We walked down the track to Plakias to catch the midday bus, and Mona was waiting there in the bus stop taverna. Michealangelo was there and all the boys, having and afternoon session. We had a coffee with Mona. She and Susanne spoke and again, I didn't grasp what was going on! The bus arrived and the new arrivals alighted, and we got on. In minutes we were off and speeding up the winding road, leaving the tree-lined road to Plakias, the pebble beach, behind us and the disco across from the surfers hostel. The bus soon reached Stavros, turned and stopped and only I got off! As I did, I saw Mona hide under a seat by the bus window, so she couldn't be seen from the taverna! The engine soon revved into action and Susanne rushed to open the window. (Moma and Nikos looked on and waved; they were well used to departures) I held Susanne's hand, as she lent down and I kissed her goodbye. I walked along with the moving bus and her hand slid out of mine. She looked back, waving, and the bus disappeared up the road, with Susanne and Mona on their way home!

That evening I sat alone at the bar and Nikos gave me a glass of red wine on the house. I was silent and quiet and sipped the wine and stared at the Irish punt, which was pinned to the bar shelf, among all the other currencies. After eating some of Moma's meatballs and chips, followed by her cinnamon rice pudding, which Susanne loved, my thoughts returned to my drawing, the Irish boat builders and the river. I looked at, and studied, the paintings on the wall, and watched Popa fall asleep beside the Wee Man. who was drinking with the priest. Moma came, sat and cracked jokes with them, and now and then, she would turn to me and say "Where's Susanne, Brendan?"

"Gone back to Bremen!" I would reply.

The Source of the River

I had thoughts of working on the olives and inquired about it. I knew that Susanne was on a train somewhere in Yugoslavia, and that eventually, she would phone and at some point, I would be compelled to go and see her. I didn't then know, that I would stand under Roland, the medieval knights statue, there in the beautiful square in Bremen, and that he would become a symbol of my hopes, and an example to everyone who strived and endured, for he had come through everything, even time. But for now, I would only think of Crete and its rivers, its people, the black nets in which dreams are caught, and its haunting music, which nearly turned me to tears.

When Charles Henry and his wife Marlene came into the taverna for a beer, they sat at my table and said hello. Almost immediately, they asked, together "Tomorrow, Brendan, would you be our guide and take us up the river to the waterfalls, and we'll go with you to find it's source!"

"Of course I will, I'd love to!" I replied, with relish, as my spirits lifted. In my brooding over Susanne, I had almost forgotten about one of the tasks I had yet to complete!

"Is it too far?" "How long will it take?" Asked Marlene.

"Oh, about a days journey there and back, not too long!" I assured her. We told stories all evening long until late. It was easy in Nikos's to stay up until 3 am without realising the time, and apparently, without ill effects. The English couple, the Milnes, were absent. He was probable writing and painting, while his wife knitted, or he was still building his aeroplane! Charles Henry had a good sense of humour and we hit it off okay. Out here in Crete, as the Irish writer used to say "You get the best people from every country", so in a way, you received and exaggerated picture of such places. I told anecdotes of my experiences at Covent Garden opera House, and some television studio stories, of Con and Bill the two Irish painters. How one would slip off under the car park for a pint, and his best friend would sing a piece from one of the great operas, as he painted along. How Con had said to me "One day Brendan, you will write a book about us!" Then, of Abdul in Goods Inwards, the writer and Peter the comic... I told Henry and Marlene but maybe they didn't see the humour, though A. Milne did! One day I had stepped out into the street from the direction of the donkey path, when I saw a man standing outside Nikos's and staring at me. "Hello, Brendan" he said. He was a rich cleaner from Television London!

"What a small world!" I said. And I longed for money.

The morning afterwards, Charles Henry, Marlene and I with rucksacks on our backs, set off in search of the source of the river. It was unusually hot, and we were happy as we could be, all going in the same direction. The valley was abuzz with crickets. Sometimes, at night, the donkeys would UUUAAHHH, and then those funny hairy animals would cry like babies. As we left the hostel, a Greek kid had a big cricket cupped in his hands. He was giggling to some other children, as the insect repeated it castanette-like clapping sound. Then, we reached the path down to the mill, and made for the river-way on the opposite side of the river. It was a lovely day and full of joyfull things and stuff.

Marlene was slightly plump, twenty two years old, just married, fit and with fair hair. Charles was a couple of years older, with a wry smile. He had a witty and swift turn of phrase, whereas Marlene was mostly silent, letting him do all the talking. Yet, she could rule the nest, and he was constantly looking after the needs and wishes. The three of us were getting on very well, on that particular day and as we reached the second waterfall, Charles helped her fix the strap on her sandle. She had firm tanned thighs and strong looking calves from hiking. By now, the rock and boulders were becoming larger and larger and more difficult to climb. The river trees bigger and older. The springs from the waterfall thundered and then softened into the deep pools. We spent all day climbing, walking and stopping for rests, with the birds singing and the crabs dashing under the rocks. The scent from the flowers and vegetation was fragrant and all the colours had that pastel tint you will only find here in Crete. We stood on enormous boulders and looked back down the river at the waterfalls and sheer drops below us. At a certain point there seemed to be no way forward, until we found a slight gap between two boulders.

Walking to the river.
The Discovery of the source of the river.

We got through with a struggle and almost got stuck between the rocks. At the other side were more rocks and more pools, and as we climbed Charles said, the sweat trickling down his brow! 'Is there no end to it?' Marlene moaned "I have to rest, my feet are sore!"

Time had gone so quickly and it was already 6 pm so we stopped for a rest.

Marlene lay on her sleeping bag, on a sandy patch near a boulder and rested her back against it. Charles gave her a carton of fruit juice and some cheese and biscuits. Though the day was still hot up above us, down here by the river, it was much cooler. Eating made us feel better but we decided to call it a day. I lead them up along a concealed path to the road. We returned to the hostel late and ate, and had an early night. The next day, we would try and find a different approach to the river. It was another beautiful night and there was a full moon. I fell asleep to the distant sound of music coming from the taverna below, and what sounded like bangs or motorcars back-firing! There were the human-like sighs of those little animals (whose name I didn't know) who leap from tree to tree. I missed Susanne, but I was content to fall into a deep relaxed sleep.

The following day we walked up the road towards the war-memorial, and Charles asked me, "Which way are we going Brendan?"

"I think that I know a better way, you'll see!"

I took them down by the small chapel, along a dirt road,which went above and parallel to the river. It didn't seem to lead anywhere, in any direction, but I followed my hunch and guided them through the trees and rocks, well up the gorge below the olive trees, which grew in rows on terraces, all up the valley. When we reached, what I expected to be, the upper reaches of the river, the river-bed was dry with bushes growing in it. Strange though this was, in a dusty and dry landscape, I continued the search and guided Charles and Marlene back down the dry river bed. After some hours, walking along this inhospitable terrain, we came to some gigantic boulders, which were completely blocking our way. A huge wall of stone stood before us, grey and hot. Somehow, we managed to climb up and over this rockface and to our surprise on the other side, were more and more of these rocks, with huge trees growing from the craggs. It was somehow get-

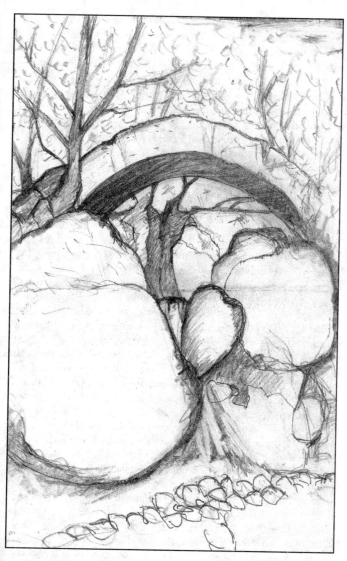

The secret bridge over the river & the blue rock Thrush.

ting cooler! Then I heard Marlene shouting ahead of us "Charles Henry, Brendan, come quickly!" We climbed forwards as fast as we could, and then we heard the wonderous sound of falling water. We reached the top of a huge boulder, to see Marlene standing on the beach of a big, blue pool looking up at a gigantic waterfall, made of three huge streams of water, which were gushing in great torrents into the bottomless pool, out of the rockface! It was coming from under the ground! That was why we couldn't find the upper part of the river. It was subterranean! Charles and I climbed down to her and we waded into the pool. We all smiled and Marlene said "So this is the source of the river!"

After a couple of hours relaxing and gazing at the waters, we decided to go back down the river. After a long time climbing down, and exploring the various caverns, pools and the wooded areas along the river, we arrived at a large patch of trees and bushes. Because of the fresh water, the vegetation grew well here, along and across the stream. Then all of a sudden, there appeared in front of us a big bridge with a beautiful waterfall. This was the second bridge across the river. It was very old and joined the two ancient donkey paths, one which led to Sellia and the other to Upper Stavros; Lower Stavros I had yet to find! It seems that the new village had been build higher up the valley, to get out of the reach of pirates from the sea?... It was a beautiful place with sunlight coming through the trees and making dazzling shapes in the fall and pool. The bridge was still intact, and completely hidden by the trees from view of the river bank and the road above. I made a sketch of this classic view and then we continued down the river, hardly talking at all, only enjoying our surroundings. The river narrowed and the vegetation thickened until there was hardly anyway through. Then we saw, for the first time, a second mill! It was ruined and covered in creepers and the top of the tower had fallen off into the river bed, blocking the way. It had that atmosphere you get in old stories about Inca temples in the jungle, and at some time, the whole valley must have had hundreds of people working down there. Going up and down through the olive groves and along numerous donkey paths. Now it was a place to camp out and get away from it all! We climbed over the tower top, which must have fallen over in a storm, and made our way over the upturned roots of big trees, which had fallen over, in the winter floods from the mountains. The floods moved everything, so the whole appearance of the

The Artist and his Blue-Bird.

river landscape was completely altered; trees pulled out by the roots, rocks turned over by the streams and landslides. When the rain poured, whole parts of the mountain roads would fall over the side of the ravines, but fortunately here earthquakes were mere tremours! After this part of the river, its stream widened and the whole valley came into view, and suddenly we were out in the open again, though still cut off enough to be out of reach, and away from the other people for as long as we desired! Before long we reached the first waterfall and Mona's cave and then the first bridge and the mill below Stavros. Henry and Marlene visited the Holy Grotto and I watched them. I went and sat on the bridg and wondered what Susanne was doing. For a brief moment I glimpsed the blue bird whistling in the trees by the stream.

Later, they joined me on the bridge and we crossed over to the mill, and climbed the path to Stavros. When we reached the road, we went down to the Tap Shop for a Nescafe. Cape Kakomouri had some white clouds drifting over it's back, and Plakias sea was full of bathers and windsurfers. The weather was good, and the evening would be too.

The hostel was full and the taverna had many new faces. Susanne phoned, she was back in her farmhouse and when I told her that I would come to see her, she said "Not yet, Brendan, its too soon!" I had been teaching Susanne English, and so she sometimes cepied my little phrases, so when I asked her on the phone - how she was? - She said, "Oh, I'm completely fucked!" Moma and Nikos seemed pleased that our romance was still going. Moma niggled "Whose been phoning you, Brendan?" and I laughed with her. Marianna came and sat at the bar near me and Moma kept a close eye on her.

"Where have you been, Marianna?" I asked her politely and cautiously.

"I have been to Hawaii. There I met a rich film director, who invited me to his house in Los Angeles!" she said boastingly.

"Now I am making much money painting murals there in his big mansion,"

"Oh, really?" I said to her as if I believed every word, which I did! Nikos smiled at me, with a twinkle in his eye, as if to say, If you believe that you will believe anything! For a moment I almost was convinced, but I had heard Marianna's fantasies before... she left, singing to herself, like a little innocent girl la la la.," She was likeable in a way. Then Nikos said "How's Mr Brendan today?"

"Fantastic!" I answered. He went around to the kitchen to help with supper. Michealangelo came into Nikos's in a friendly mood, then the Wee Man, then a crowd of local men, and some guys from another village, who liked to play cards for money. Soon the back packers came down from the hostel for supper, and later the couples, who rented holiday rooms, who came to have private conversations, and early, the Milnes and the English couple who lived in Athens, the sort who never wanted to go back to the cold. I was introduced, and they were a likeable civilised couple, though the old man ate his pudding - ice cream like a little boy. Then we were joined by a silver-haired Irish lady and her husband, who drove his jeep like a madman, and he said to me that there was no money in art, and I agreed with him, pointing out that I had no illusions about the subject, and that my financial state was somewhat precarious. I had sold half my paints to Mr Milne and a watercolour to a young English businessman from London, who had cut my price. I had even given away my painting of Bridge over Troubled Waters to Susanne, but that was a gift of love.

Lunchen on the Grass by Manet;
The Scottish Model Couple in the Egyptian Holiday Brochure.

Michealangelo told us stories about the partisan caves and of old Stavros, located down the valley.

The next day, Charles Henry and Marlene left and gave me their sleeping mat. I remembered how, the year before, when I had been painting the hostel wall, with Cecile, they had come and given me a pint of beer. It was stinking hot and they said that it was the custom in their town, to give painters a drink like this. They were so kind and it made me so happy. On that same evening, the Scottish couple returned from Egypt. The woman had bright ginger hair, and the man, a moustache, and a brushed-back Valentino hair style. They had been walking along a street in Cairo, when a manager of a hotel had come out to them saying "Would you like some work?" They thought washing up! But they ended up in the Bridalsuite, as guests of the management with trips up the Nile. Everything was free of charge. Their faces were splashed all over the companies brochure. They looked as odd as the reclining figures in Manets-Luncheon on the Grass. They spent three weeks like this and couldn't believe their luck! The funny thing was (as they realised at the time) they didn't at all look like the typical English holiday couple. They were married, but that was the only resemblance. They were totally incongruous together, photographically and visually, though not so as a happy pair! But to the Egyptian hotelier, they were exactly what he wanted! They left for Egypt as I arrived and now as they returned, I was about to leave, what we both considered home. We said that we now had two homes, one here in Stavros, Crete, and one somewhere else! You always met such nice people here in the village because the ones who loved it, stayed.

I met Marianna in a cafe by the disco the next day, and she showed me a photo of her on a peepshow poster; she looked good. She bought me a coffee and we talked. Marianna said, "You have a new girlfriend, I saw you with her in the Tap-shop," Marianna said in a playful way, laughing.

"Yes Marianna, I love her!" I answered seriously.

"But you were with that English girl before," she said accusatively,

"You're always with a new woman!"

"Not always!" I replied.

"I'm going to Bremen, to see her tomorrow, I can't wait any longer!" Marianna smiled "You'll never change, Brendan!", you're like me!" It was another beautiful day, as I walked up the donkey path to the village, past the black nets and away from the sea.

The sky was clear and the walls of the houses hurt my eyes, with the intensity of the light, as the sun touched everybody and everything around. The bright colours stood out on the doors and windows. I had a farewell party with the Milnes, the English couple I liked so much. He told me the story of the Australian no-hoper, and we laughed. I was happy that I was going to see Susanne, but at the same time, sad to leave the village. I wished that we could all be together in the same place. I talked to the English businessman, so as to prepare myself for the realities ahead of me in Northern Europe, and to come gently out of "Dream Time", away from the dream nets! The next day I left in a car, after a last drink with the Scottish couple. We drove off and they waved goodbye. In Germany, it would be wonderful, and then tragic, and in Holland, a lost friend would sing to me, Christy Moore's - "Don't forget your shovel if you want to go to work!" I thought to myself, until the next time! Nikos said sadly, Mr Brendan is leaving! "What will we do without you?"

Part Four

Winter

I got off the bus in the dark, and just managed to find my way up the road towards Stavros. I was the only one to do so, as if I were stopping at some isolated place. The bus drove off, leaving me there at the side of the road, with only my rucksack and a slight moon to give me a grip on reality. I was full of anticipations, excited and wondered what my reception would be? Returning to the source of my inspiration. I felt alone, but determined to carry through my plan. I walked up the tarmac surface, the landscape of trees was dark umber in hue and a chilly breeze blew the wild branches. At last I came to the village. It was dead quiet and pitch dark, but there were bright lights shining out of the houses. I quickly passed Nikos's taverna and I caught his eye as I did; the door was open and the inside was all lit up. He was serving behind the bar. He had a serious expression and the winter light made his hair and moustache look much darker. I went upstairs and left my baggage and promptly returned to the bar. I made straight for a bar stool, and he gave me a welcoming Raki. Still wound up from travelling, I hardly noticed the people and the insular scene behind me in the taverna. "How is your luck?" Nikos asked me, kindly. "Okay", I replied in a non-detailed manner, "Some good, some bad". "Where is the German woman, Susanne?" Nikos inquired. "In Germany, working," I answered. He gave me another drink and I noticed and old enemy, a malcontent from the north of England, sitting at a table reading a book. I wasn't glad to see him, but it didn't matter, and anyway, maybe he and things had changed. After a few drinks I relaxed, as Nikos had earlier suggested to me "Relax, Mr. Brendan!" "Siga, siga!"

The taverna had some minor alterations - a domed hatch in one of the semipartitions, which separated the two taverna areas. Now Nikos could view all parts of the place from the bar. There were some new water-colours on the walls. One I noticed was very professional, but

too photographic for my liking. The others were pleasant but ama-
teurish. Obviously in the past year, while I had been away, various
other artists had passed through the village. The big sombreros and
the banknotes had been moved, but the eagles and hawks were still
there on the wall. The stove was installed for winter, and its metal
chimney pipe, twisted up along the wall, and bent out through a hole
in the glass window into the street. Every now and then, the wind
would gush through the gap between the glass and the tinpipe. As in
my first visit to the taverna, Moma had left the big copper kettle boiling steadily, and it would once in a while, hiss with steam and gurgle
as the kettle lid jumped up and down. Everybody would stop what
they were doing and Nikos and I would chuckle, while the Greeks
smiled and the travellers sneered with a start as they looked in the direction of the stove. The place was so laid-back, and I was out of tune
with its relaxed state, after my quixotic struggles and leaping about in
England, Holland and Germany. I was full of stress and confusion
and I had come home as a desperate measure, after failures in love
and money, to try and clear my head, and do some winter pictures.
For the moment, I had a reprieve, from what I then thought was to be
the final denouement. This time I had just made it to Nikos's by the
skin of my teeth!

I was looking at the new painting on the wall, when Nikos said "We
thought that you would be here in the summer. Marianne was asking
for you!" "I couldn't come, I was working in Germany and Holland!"
Later, Mr. Milne noticed how worried I was, and he said to me "Your
problem is, Brendan, that you are an emotional decision-maker! I had
the same trouble when I was young and then someone had a good talk
with me. You've got to get an income, and you've got to think things
out". Mr. Milne had popped into Nikos's in his usual manner. He
would suddenly appear through the door, like Harry Worth in his
white suit, just to see who was around, make a delightful impromptu
turn-about walk, and then suddenly make his exit. He was surprised
to see me and when he did he said "You keep turning up like a bad
penny, Brendan!" Then he said in a friendly way "I'll be back later.
Cheers!" I really liked him and his wife, like old-friends. Yet, we had
only known each other for several weeks in all, and all of that in
Crete. I'm sure he thought that I was an incurable dreamer, and everything was mostly my own fault! He said that I would have to change
my technique. Referring to Susanne, he warned "Someone else will

Nikos's Bar, Stavros village.

have her, Brendan! You'll disappear like the Dinosaurs!" In his way he advised, amused and helped me.

Some things were good, and some things were bad. The good thing was - I was in Stavros with friends, with some art-materials, and the beginnings of a travel book. If I been through all the seasons of Crete, without leaving, I'm sure I wouldn't have loved the palace so much. This way, I had glimpsed most of the seasons and had involuntary left! (Mona had said to me that we should transform lifes limitations into advantages). Though I had never seen the brightest time in Crete, the Spring, when everything blooms!, I had experienced the good place from all different kinds of angles, and at tangents.

That night I slept well, and in the morning I woke to the bright sun, the sun of an English summer, the sun of a Cretan winter by a warm sea, with 'short' days and long evenings, with sudden storms, light-ning and thunder, with power-cuts, when the electricity cables fell from the old wooden posts. Mr. Milne and I would watch the cracking bursts of sparks, as the rain hit the poletops in the dark evening. Sometimes, there would be freak snow-storms, and once, while we all sat in the taverna, there was a sudden deluge of large hailstones, which hit the restaurant windows with bullet-like ferocity. Only the African winds really lasted long. The downpours of rain cleared up withing hours, with a full rainbow clearly visible above the valley of olive trees, and the sun would be out again. Winter was Moma's bean-soup, the kettle boiling on the taverna stove, the evenings clos-ing in and the surprisingly cool nights. The Weeman playing cards with his mates, the Cretan young man with Afro hair, the empty shores of Plakias, and swimming in the warm sea, the olive-pickers waiting around in Lefkoyia village, the dark blue, skies, colder col-ours in the landscape and warmer feelings inside, and the winter trav-ellers looking for work and solace.

That night Mr Milne introduced me to the American writer, who had come there to create his short-stories. He lived in a flat at the back of Nikos's overlooking Cape Kakomouri. He was well mannered and a gentleman from the South. He had a natural humility which cloaked his talents and intelligence. All of us would play cards for small amounts of money. He would always keep sober - I guessed so that he would have a clear head for his writing. He arrived in Nikos's taverna at the same time each evening for dinner..

Winter begins.

Wrapped Van.

One day, I went to visit him at his invitation but he was out. His typewriter had a sheet of white paper in it. and two sheets of a short story lay on his writing desk. There was a large double-bed and many books. He had trouble sleeping because, after an easy year out here in Crete, he now had to return home to the United States. He had a job waiting, but I supposed that he wanted to carry on with his stories. I looked at the pages of his pages of his story and then left.

A Short Story by Golli Michael Egan

Showing off those legs, those perfect legs. Fearful of the image, the power of the vamp, the fascinating prestige of her racing body. A regal start filtered dripping though. The hint of pleasure. The private knowledge. The menace of her body surfaced. In capsules of discrete significance, in intervals of digital space she lived with this woman. In small doses.

In the bathroom, a stained glass head floated in the mirror. Water splashed everywhere in an effort to remove it. Buttoning up his shirt, he recognized the mask as his own. Through the ravers, squeezing past a weave of jittering faces she swore revenge in a frenzy of modesty. Revenge on her scrambled lover, a ghost dissolved in the present. A suction pump vacating all echo of the future, pumping wildly capsizing her ambition.

In the hour before the property book chimed in Clifton and Finsbury Park they clashed in the sickled beetle. He felt pain and yammered, she barked him out of the car, throat cracking. He laboured with his coat. Then bloodshot eyes accelerated. Swerving down streets of comfortable decay. Braking hard at a barrier of steel scaffold ready to decapitate. The blue sheath stammed. The automobile would not come to life again.

The few times we had made it love was not what we made. We may have been there or I may have been in love with the smothered discipline exacted by infatuation. From whatever position in space it became an approximation of a counterfeit act. An encounter with a charged bar ascending and descending, its course traced with a circular key. When the key touched the bar a bell shrieked and she froze tepid.

I never slept, I never woke, I left a hamstrung smile. Backward to another bed. A room aboard a junk shop. I tested all for comfort, burning a hollow in the mattress. I turned away from the thrashing of a night which had allowed no shade.

Turning, mesmerised, his gaze fastened to a window, barred and al

The dinasaur awakes

most opaque with the dust of life. A grey sky drew closer forching his head beneath the blankets. Eyes adapt to the dark, pigment is reborn. In the melting clouds at the spare end of dawn, through the insect dead window, he watched again a grainy mosaic of cells rustle and bleach. (After having been exposed to the light the animal was immediately decapitated. The eye was the removed and cut open along the equator, and the rear half of the eyeball containing the retina laid in a solution).

The following day Maria at work in the clinic showed a colleague a clear optograph on the retina of the murdered eye, a pattern of flaking painted bars in tamed rhodopsin......

Later that afternoon, I met Mr. Milne and his wife Bet, and the writer, and we went for a long drive up over the mountains towards Frango-kastello. The panoramic views were indescribably beautiful, but impossible to photograph because the Cameras eye couldn't take everything in at once. Only the human 'eye' could do this, or perhaps the many dimensional, imaginative canvas of the painter. Even a grid system of photographs wasn't quite right. You could take hundreds of shots and put them all together, but it still didn't give you what you saw. We stopped and Mr. Milne and I did some sketching on a small beach with one taverna. It was good to have a friend like him.

Afterwards, we made for Stavros, stopped for a few minutes there, and drove off for Spili. It always amazed me how totally different each village and valley was from the other! It was getting towards twilight and there was a downpour of rain. As we drove up the hills, we could see the grey rainclouds burst forth all over the valleys and spray the trees and mountains. In other areas, the sky would be clear, with the sun shining on the grey mountains, as on the backs of elephants. (Cecile had seen the Elephants in the contours of the Hills, and I had seen the Dinosaurs). As we drove into Spili, the rain flowed along the muddy street. The place was busy and more of a small town that a village. It was drizzling now like a sun-shower. One end of Spili was getting the full effect of a rain-shower, and the other was bathed in sunshine. Mr. Milne did some shopping and then we made our way back to Stavros. He had been out here two years, and knew the place quite well. Often, artists select that which is imaginatively interesting, so I sometimes had a different interpretation of the place than he, perhaps even a more confined and limited one, though later these perceptions would be digested into a broader view. Often travellers and tourists had only passing glimpses of the island and saw only the tourist places.

We reached Nikos's and separated. My holiday was over, and soon, in the next week, I would have to go to Lefkoyia in search of work. It was grim in the cold hostel, as was my precarious state. All the romance had gone. The American writer described to me how there had been a great conflagration, caused by a falling electric-cable. It nearly destroyed the whole valley, Plakias, Stavros and everything. The Army came and everyone came out to fight the fire. It had burned its way half up the valley and raged for three days, day and night, and everyone had packed to leave. When all hope of stopping the fire had gone, the wind suddenly changed direction, and the valley was saved.

I washed and changed and went downstairs to the taverna at about eight-o'clock. I looked inside and it was choc-a-bloc with villagers. The bar was vacant and Nikos was there behind it, fiddling about with some infernal machine. I had my back to what looked like a cinema audience and as I spoke to Nikos, everyone shouted at me in Greek "Get out of the Fecken way!", and I returned the compliment! Nikos pointed to the wall, and I gasped with angry amazement! Right before my eyes was a colour television screen with a video! I pushed my

View of Stavros village from the Power Station.

way through the seated crowd to the back of the restaurant where some young Greens were sitting, in hope of peace and quiet, and we consoled each other. The monster had reached Crete! Luckily, there was Nikos who always reached a point of boredom. So for about three weeks there would be video films all day and evening and then suddenly, it was turned off all the time. The music and conversation was back, and we could all be human again. In fact, it was bad for business, as traveller and tourist alike had come to get away from videos and discos, and enjoy good food, fresh air and human-contact.

When Susanne phoned I was happy, and I was getting into the winter experience, which was a good contrast to the other seasons. Often, the place was so interesting that there was no great need to paint or write about it; it was enough to live it. Otherwise, you were wasting time being a voyeur, when you should have been living for the day! One afternoon, when I had been work-hunting around Lefkoyia, I met a graphic-designer who was on a three month trip. He was the only English-speaker among a crowd of young French people, whe were trying to 'get on' the olives. One of this group, a Corsican, stood out, with his knowledge of languages, and his rapport and repartee with the villagers. Sadly, he had become a token-Greek. He was well-in, and he knew all about what work was going in the area. He continuously conversed in the Cretan dialect with the locals. He never left the village. He was good natured and helped everyone, especially those who had run out of money 'graduating' from tourist to foreign-labourer. One young Frenchman said to me with bitterness "I will never do this again in my life!" Unfortunately, foreign labour cut the going rate of pay for the locals so they were understandably not too happy about it. Most of these French kids spoke no English, and the local Greeks spoke Cretan and German, so it was difficult for me to get what was going on. What made things worse was that we were all competing with each other for work.

The olive-harvest hadn't started because the farmers were waiting until the rain stopped, weighed down the olives on the trees, and then they would be picked. There were small trees and big trees, and each had a different harvesting time. While I waited for some work, I chatted with the graphic-designer and told him my story, how if I failed to get work and save, I would surely lose Susanne, and any chance of writing or painting, but he advised me that often in life good comes

Waiting for the olive-harvest in Lefkoyia.

out of bad luck and you get new opportunities and see new horizons. He had lost his sweetheart in Denmark, in a similar way to me. There had been no problem with their relationship, but he couldn't speak Danish and he couldn't find employment. He was brought down by circumstances outside his control and it was nothing to do with friendship or love! He said that I should go for the book and not lose hope. At the time, however, I was in a purgatorial state, as Mr. Milne pointed out, saying to me 'Didn't your father ever have a good talk to you about living in the past, and wishing things were different? You must take a decision and face the reality. You obviously don't really want to be an olive worker! You'll end up, if your not carefull cutting off your ear!" He continued - "Love is a rare gift from God. When he thinks (as Mr. Mailer points out) looking down 'That poor mother has suffered enough. Give him some love!' What's gone is gone! Yesterday is Yesterday, Brendan! Someone else will have Susanne!" Then I tried to tell him about the Continuous Past, which the Irish writer and I had experienced here in Crete and in our Ireland. The writer had said to me in my first week in the village "You and I understand Brendan!" But Mr. Milne would not listen, and he shot me down with criticism and kindness. Saying, "Everybody is out for themselves, Brendan. What are you going to do about the injustices which have been infliced upon you?" He was right! My fellow olive workers had betrayed me! But he was not to know that I was made out of a harder metal than he knew. I would get my revenge and set it all down and return like Odysseus.

It was all pretty intense stuff which occupied my head, as the graphic-designer and I drove up over the hills past Sellia village. He was determined to have a good time, and the beer, though not solving any problems, lightened my burdens so. We suddenly came to a white washed village, the sun was hot and bright, and the place looked like a Dali painting. The windows and their lattice doors were bright blue. There was a big clock on the tower of the building before us, at the side of the pebble road. The door below it, was coloured cerulean blue. In front of the door stood two men who were dressed like tramps, with beards, red faces and torn clothes. From the tower window one shouted down to us "Welcome, come in! Beer! Beer!" We stopped the car and looked up. The poorly clothed men were putting beer and snacks on a table on a first-floor roof veranda, with stone steps leading up to it. Then we both chuckled when we realized that the clock was stopped because it was painted onto the tower wall! The villagers were short of cash, so they painted a clock there. The men were friendly and we drank a few bottles on that sunny afternoon and then returned to Stavros.

Nikos didn't like this man so when he was joined by the French, I left his table and sat at the bar. Anyway, the designer was fascinated by a particular French girl. He spoke French, so he could appreciate her witty conversation. She seemed kind and friendly but her apprearance made me laugh. She was the spitting image of Popeyes girlfriend! That and her way of speaking was enough to make me split my sides. It was strange, even in my worst moments in Stavros, something funny or interesting always happened to lift me above my little problems. The English designer and the French kids didn't fit in Nikos's with their inward aspirations, so they left for, up and coming Lefkoyia where moneymaking was about to show its ugly face. The next day I would go there again to seek work.

I eventually found work with a German-speaking farmer, but the grass was too wet and it was too cold for camping out. After a few unpleasant days, I returned to Stavros, where I heard of vacancies in another village. The German speaking Cretan had been kind to me, and one lunch-break he had showed me how to cut a pipe of bamboo and make a flute. In minutes, he made one and played it to me, just like one of those ancient Greek shepherds.

It wasn't easy to be romantic working in the wet grass! One morning, I set off for a nearby village to find another farmer. I was known in Stavros so it wasn't very difficult to make contact with one, even though my Greek was minimal. I sat in the taverna and ordered a meal and beer and waited on two consecutive evenings. When we met, he said to me that he needed a few couples, the men to work the olive-picking-machines and the women to do the basket-work, picking up the olives from the nets and ground. When I told Nikos what I intended to work as he said, taking-the mick "So you're going to be a monkey, climbing trees!" Later I would find out what he really meant! and what Marcos meant when he said a year before "I hate Fecken Olives, Brendan!" "They're all money crazy around hre!" I would find out what those black nets were really for, and the rocks and baskets, which I had seen from an aesthetic point of view. With a Swedish couple, two Australian motorbikers and a man called John, I set off every morning at about 7.30 in the farmer's Datsun van. It was always cold and bright in the morning and Moma and Popa were always up before everybody else. At first, it was quite good being employed and learning a new trade. How to move the nets along under the trees, on the terraced olive fields, holding them down with stones (so that all the olives were collected) in the gushing wind. I noticed, whenever one did any manual work, that bags, boxes and other working implements were, relative to a man's strength, always just that too much too heavy to lift or carry). The olive picking machines consisted of a heavy diesel-motor with a pull-start, a pneumatic hose, which drove a series of plastic propellers. There was also, a technique of beating the olives off the trees with a stick, which the women did with great skill. The machines however, were faster for certain kinds of

The Small Mill and the fruit farm near Stavros. →

olive trees. My arms ached after a whole days working, but it was better for me than picking up the fruit and filling the baskets, as I was too tall and pigeon-toed. The farmer and his family were small and so they could leap under, on to and from tree to tree with ease. This was hell for me with my tall boney frame, and when it came down to it, a couple was needed! so a smaller (hopefully) girl-friend or wife could do the basketwork. Big old trees might have been easier for me (or for Nikos for that matter). Then I had to fill the 70 kilo sacks, load them on a donkey (if he were near enough), and take them to the Datsun van which was parked on the nearest dirt-track. As I worked along the terraces of trees, I moved the nets (flat-ground would have been much easier) and rocks and piles of sacks. We had a half-hour break at 1 pm and carried on until about 5 pm. On an hourly rate of pay it would have been okay, but we were being paid by the kilo, until the farmer decided which of us were the hardest workers. John was there to show us how and then he would be off to another job.

My heart, however, wasn't really in it, working for next to nothing, while John kept buying me drinks after work, which tired me out, I was emotionally exhausted and couldn't sleep in the cold hostel. It was a crazy situation to be in, while the Swedes and Auzzies, ironi-cally, were by no means poor, their wages being extra pocket money. So after a couple of weeks olive-picking, John and the two couples decided to accept the farmers offer to them and so dispense with any kind of solidarity.

I should have confronted them, as was suggested, but I was too tired and anyway, I didn't think that they were worth the effort. Standing down there under an olive tree, with the blair of the machine, I thought of George Orwell, and knew that everywhere was the same, competition and betrayal. (There, you forgot you were in Crete, and you could have been anywhere). But for the black-nets, the olives and rocks, I had competely forgotten about the beauty of Crete!

I was glad when we were paid, but my associates didn't tell me that I had got the sack, except for the Swedish woman who said that the farmer only wanted couples. I wondered how I had got involved with these people. It would be a long time before I touched olives again. There were some lovely girls in Nikos's and I was resigned to the fact that I must go back! When I would see Susanne again, I didn't really know and now she thought that I was a very strange man indeed!.

I got back to my art, watched the goings-on in the village, and re-membered how the little farmer laughed at my olive-picking antics as I tripped over the nets and swayed with the heavy machine. It was good to be free again. The next morning I decided to make a trip to the river to see how it all looked! I drank the red village wine, and sa-voured Moma's cooking. My black-nets were now all surrealistic in content and full of pain and disillusionment, and I played cards and passed the time.

As I walked down the path to the first mill, I thought of the plans I had for putting a Cretan windmill on the roof of the hostel. With all the wind it would be fairly easy to generate electricity. It would also have been lovely to renovate the mill, and get the water flowing again but these ideas were dreams.

When I reached the stream beyond the first bridge, I could see how the winter floods had altered everything. Boulders and trees were in different places, some pools had gone and new ones were in their place. The banks of the river were more or less the same, and it was cold, down here out of the sun. I then climbed and walked up the side of one of those winter stream beds, until I reached the path which led towards the bee farm. The way was muddy and wet, but still interest-ing. I was shocked at what I found. Beyond a certain point, above the river bank valley everything was burnt black, but surprising the bee hives were still there. There was the smell of wet charcoal and it clung to everything, but I knew that before long all would grow again because the waterfalls gushed and the river still flowed. I remembered all the good things which had happened to me here, and how I had made a written wish in the Holy grotto, asking for good luck in Love and Art and I had left-out wealth!

After some time, thinking and walking, I arrived at the second bridge. One way led to Sellia and the other to Stavros. I stood on the stone bridge and looked at the flowing stream and the waterfall. I decided to walk up a bit to Sellia and then make a turn-about tour towards the farm of fruit gardens, with its small vinyard and mill. The climb up the path under the olive trees by the nets and rocks was a silent one, until I heard the sound of an animal slipping on the gravel. I looked up the path, and saw a Woman riding on a donkey, a Boy walking by

The first Mill, near Stavros.

Olive Trees →

I moved my things to her table, sat down and greeted her with a smile. We played contentedly and she told me that she was an artist. She was a master of water-colour, calligraphy and now she was trying western landscape painting. She loved Crete! She was about thirty years old and I imagined that sometimes she could be unfathomable. When an acquaintance of mine came to our table, he promptly moved, when he saw her face implode, as she withdrew into herself. I asked her "What was the matter?" and she replied, "Sorry, I haven't been introduced to that man" she added "Oh, sometimes, I get very traditional, but it goes after a while!" "But you weren't introduced to me!" I said. "Yes but that was different, I wanted to speak to you, and also being a silly Japanese woman, I had to when I saw your sketch book. You see, I saw you before you saw me. We ladies have to be careful. My family could disown me for even the smallest reason".

Her face had lost it's mask like expression, which she wore when she wanted, to be invisible or left alone, now she was full of smiles and friendship. I hadn't yet realized that I'd found my muse again, and a new way forward!

The next day was beautiful and more like summer than winter, maybe because I was seeing everything in a different way, like that first day I had discovered the village and met new friends. The sun was shining, the trees were laden with olives, the birds were singing, there was that smell of herbs, and the sound of music coming from the travelling-shop. The Japanese woman and I went for a walk way up beyond Sellia Village. The view was breathtaking and she made some delicate pencil sketches there, by the bending roadside. On our way back she said to me "When are you leaving, Brendan?" "Oh, in a couple of days, I am getting the boat to Athens and then a bus to London, but I don't know whether to go to see my girlfriend in Germany or not, I have run out of luck and she can see no future for us!" I explained my story to Yukki, but I really wasn't sure myself what I was going to do in the next few weeks. You see, I had no fall back, and nobody to fall back upon! My only real hope was to bounce from the bottom, back up and land on my feet again, and I always managed to land on my feet somehow! Susanne wanted to see me, but only if I were independent!

As we walked back to Stavros, there was a strong wind blowing, and Yukki wore a white raincoat. She carried her sketchbook under one arm, and I held her hand. It was an unusual experience to be with such a foreign woman in this country setting. The coat she wore was much too big and I had to keep turning up the sleeves, over her delicate hands. Her long black hair blew all over the place, and she said for her loudly, because of the sound of the wind.

"It's so beautiful" "What?!" "I asked, putting my hand to my ear to listen and leaning towards her. "IT'S SO BEAUTIFUL!!" she shouted into my ear, making me jerk. "YES IT IS!" I replied, and we both laughed and continued down towards the village.

That evening we ate together and small portions were enough for her because of her size. We exchanged addresses and she taught me a little of her language.

"Will you come back to Crete?" she asked me.
"Yes I will return! It's the best place I've ever been!"
She had a wide knowledge and we discussed many things, and since she was an artist, we had a lot in common. We compared notes, and impressions of the people and landscape of the island.

Olive trees.

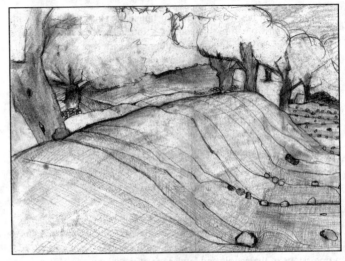

Working on the olive-nets.

"Will you visit me in England?" she asked me, formally.
"Yes, I will" I replied, accepting her invitation.

After several games of backgammon we made a short walk under a full moon. I noticed how petite she was, and I couldn't believe my eyes how black her hair was, so I touched it, to make sure that it was real! It was soft and deep ivory-black, with a moon-sheen, its blackness making her coloured lips seem redder than they really were. She wore a purple flower of Crete in the dark strands by her ear, and it reminded me of the Spring to come! and its multitudes of plants and flowers.

Yukki's map of Crete.

As we stood gazing, she looked out at Cape Stavros, the moon sinking into the sea of dark blue and she turned and said to me,
Kureta dai Suki, Criti Suga puo,

Je t'aime,
Eu te amo,
Seri sevigarum,
Te quiero,
Ik hau van jou,
Ich liebe dich,
Ti amo,
Mo ghra Thu,
I love you!

et cetera, et cetera!...........................

Crete and Yukki never ceased to surprise me!

Images of Crete

Cecile danced with Georgio
On a coal black Cretan night.
The mountains were disappearing
with the day;
Nikos blinked his eyes beneath his
black moustache,
And held her tight, the Lyra sighing.

The Weeman played Dominoes with the Canadian,
Silently watching the red moon
Going down in the bay.
Big-Jim said - Show us your beard!
As he poured a bucket of water
Over Edith Piaf - who just laughed
As she filled another glass of Whisky.

A boat sailed over the flat Aegean Sea;
Black nets clung to olive trees.
The painter put his brushes away,
Mo, the artists model, was still,

Marianna was down on her knees by the Grotto.
Ilona was down by the mill.
Old George was having his hair cut,
Granny was watering the plants on the windowsill,
Moma was watching the till, and
Popa and Father Murphy were half-asleep on the Taverna table.
As Old Father Time from the Boreen, approached
Mirthios, the Kettle was free.
The ordinary was extraordinary.
While a fire blazed around Preveli Monastry,

the Partisan flashed his gold teeth; as
A woman, a man, and a boy on a donkey
Made their way up the goat-path
Through the Olive Trees.

The Road to Damnoni and Amondi Beaches.
Lefkoyia

The stopped clock at Stavros.

The donkey path to Stavros.

Views around Plakias.

Views around Plakias.

Views around Plakias.

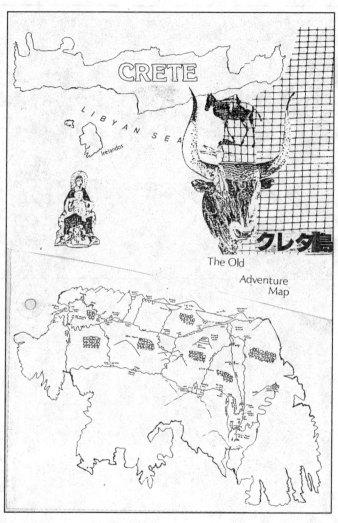

The Old Adventure map.

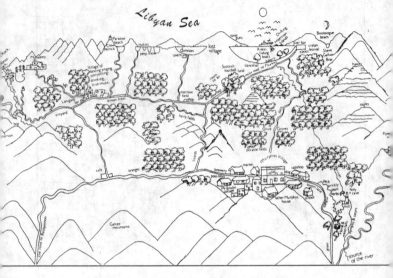

The Adventure Map.

CONTENTS

PART THREE

PART FOUR